THE SEA WAS KIND

LIEUTENANT YOUNG AND THE AUTHOR (*left*) ON THEIR ARRIVAL IN AUSTRALIA

Contents

v

Illustrations

Author's Foreword

A FIRST draft of this book—including the present title —was made early in 1944, but wartime censorship did not release it until later.

The story is factual and was mainly taken from a diary and log kept by me between 8th December 1941 and 15th December 1942. When information came to me second-hand, I have said so.

In describing the two boat voyages, many islands and small places have been mentioned. Some of these are not likely to be found on any but large-scale maps and charts of the Philippine Islands, and of the area between them and the north coast of Australia. However, the two track charts included here will make it easy to follow the story.

A. K.

Melbourne.

I. TO MANILA

JAPAN

THE flight from Sydney to Tokyo had been very smooth so far. The great silver Super Constellation cruised effortlessly at 14,000 feet. Beautiful hostesses came round with beautiful drinks just before lunch. They did you well on Qantas Flight EM 234.

We had left Mascot aerodrome, Sydney, the evening before and had cruised two thousand miles through the still night diagonally across the Australian Continent to Darwin, arriving in the early hours of the morning. After a refreshing bath and breakfast at "Berimah", the Qantas hostel, we set off on the lap to Manila, flying north across the Arafura Sea and the Moluccas. By noon we were well over the Philippines cruising in sunshine above broken white clouds and I was in a state of happy drowsiness induced by the luxurious armchair and the quiet humming of the big engines.

Then I saw it. Below us, through a break in the cloud cover, I saw the northern coast of Mindanao and, some fifty miles farther north, the south coast of Negros. This was the stretch of water on which many years ago I had tried to battle my way north-eastwards across the Mindanao Sea. I was single-handed in a twenty-four-foot boat and trying desperately to escape from the Japanese who were pouring down to occupy the Philippine Islands. But I had struck the wrong time of year with head winds all the time, and although I managed to sail about twenty miles in a day, I was thrown back almost as far while I slept until, at last, after a week of battling, I had to give up and work out a new plan of escape to Australia.

Now the clouds closed in again, the vision below disappeared, and I was back in the cabin of the Constellation.

The story really started in Germany, where I was born a year before the outbreak of the First World War. My father was a manufacturer, and I had been educated in the seaport of Hamburg where people liked to play with boats and ships of all sizes.

But in 1933 a little Austrian house painter came to power in Germany and things changed rapidly after that. Hitler decided that my family were not really Aryans, whatever that meant. Although we could trace their residence in Germany back to the seventeenth century, like millions of others, we lost everything, and in 1935, at the ripe old age of twenty-one, I became a refugee.

After spending a week in London I went to Japan. It was not permitted to take much in money or valuables out of Germany, but I was able to scrape up enough for a third-class fare in a Japanese ship to Japan. My bunk was in a six-berth cabin, way aft by the propeller shaft and deep down in the ship and although, since then, I have travelled in luxury cabins, I have never enjoyed myself quite as much as I did during the five weeks voyage on the SS. "Haruna Maru" from London to Kobe. Everything was new and I had the strength and optimism that is rooted in ignorance.

Unlike others with a similar background, who walk through life with a permanent chip on their shoulder, my refugee status never worried me. It did not take long to discover that the people to whom the word "refugee" was something of a dirty word, were ill-mannered or ignorant folk who didn't matter anyway. I was young, and the world was a most interesting place.

I chose Japan for no particular reason other than that I knew someone who knew someone else in that country who might get me a job. Moreover, the Far East had always interested me and conditions in Japan for small-

2

boat sailing were reputed to be ideal. So I went to Kobe to a job with an import and export firm, and I have followed the same trade ever since.

Although I arrived in Japan four years after the Manchurian Affair and Japan's exit from the League of Nations, life between 1935 and 1938 was pleasant enough, and the people I had to do with were hard working, kindly and had a sense of humour. After struggling for a year or two with the language, I could speak Japanese well enough to make myself understood, and this added greatly to my enjoyment when I went exploring. Japan is a land of great and varied natural beauty and I did a lot of hiking around the countryside; and each year, after skiing in January in the mountainous north, I never failed to get a tremendous thrill when I returned to the warmer regions of the south-west and saw the first plum blossoms among bare trees and empty paddy fields.

Yachting was my passion. I owned a little twenty-one-foot sloop, double ended, built of stout teak. Her not very original name was "Spray", and in her I spent my off-duty hours and days between March and December. Japan was, indeed, the ideal country for sailing, a yachtsman's paradise.

In 1939, after four years, my brother Eric had followed me to Japan fresh from a short spell in one of Hitler's "protective custody" camps, then the polite name for concentration camps. He, too, became an enthusiastic yachtsman and together we were a good team. We explored hundreds of small islands and coastal nooks on the Inland Sea, that stretch of deep water enclosed by the main island of Honshu and by Shikoku and Kyushu Islands. On summer evenings we would put into a small port after a hard day's sail and Japanese fishing-smacks would come alongside and sell us some of their fresh catch. Then we would make fast for the night and go ashore to exchange small talk with the fishermen, about wind and weather, currents and tides, as small-boat sailors and fishermen do all over the world.

3

We collected books on yachting, and the names of the giants among small-boat sailors became household words. There was Captain Voss of the "Tillikum", the inevitable Captain Joshua Slocum and his "Spray", Claud Worth and the greatest of them all, Captain Bligh of the "Bounty". I admired Captain Bligh extravagantly.

The social life of bachelors in Japan was concentrated mostly in the clubs, which had an English atmosphere and were mainly inhabited by Englishmen. I liked the life and became infatuated with everything British—a feeling that was to grow with the years; but at this time it was largely the hunger of the boy looking in from the outside.

On the day in 1935, when I had stepped off the train in London I had a curious feeling of being at home. The British way of life was solid and enduring; it stood for political freedom and respect for the privacy of the individual. Coming from the Germany of the thirties, these ideals were very real to me then, as they are now. British people had passports which opened just about every door around the globe—I did not even have a passport after mine became valueless—and they accepted me into their clubs and houses without reserve, and for that I was grateful.

If the social life in pre-war Japan was idyllic, the political life was not. The clouds were gathering quickly.

In Japan, as in Germany, the same forces were at work, perverting the instincts and abilities of a whole people. Patriotism, that fine sentiment of pride in one's country and its history, was distorted into an aggressive dogma of superiority and intolerance. Thus a virtue was turned into a vice by the teachings of the "gunbatsu", the militarist clique who exploited for their own ends a people still steeped in feudalism.

The parallel with Germany was very compelling, and I found it difficult to see how anyone could believe in Pacific peace after Hitler struck in 1939.

Hitler started his war on a Sunday. The next morning I presented myself at the British Consulate in Kobe to ask whether I could be enlisted in the British Forces. British men of my age had begun to leave Japan in droves for enlistment in Hong Kong, Singapore and Australia. Why not I? It was my war just as much as theirs; I had already lost more than most of them. The Consul, Mr. Hubert Graves, was an understanding man and he was terribly nice to me, but the answer was a polite "no". There was simply no precedent for enlisting a man of my doubtful national status. In fact, I had no nationality at all.

I kept pestering him and his office while the gangsters in Japan gained ground steadily and life became more and more unpleasant as the whole economy of the country was geared for war. Unseen guns supplanted butter, and the ties of friendship formed between foreigners and Japanese were torn under the strain of more and more overt anti-white propaganda.

It was on a Sunday afternoon late in June 1941, when we had just returned from a week-end yachting trip along the west coast of Awaji Island in "Spray", that we heard the news of Hitler's attack on Russia. Awaiting us at our buoy in the yacht basin was our boatswain, his kindly old face haggard, and all he could stammer was "Senso"—war. Ignorant as he was of politics, he understood that the stab at Russia meant the way was clear for a Japanese move southward, and for war with Britain and America.

Early the next month at an Imperial conference in Tokyo the Emperor, his hand forced by his military advisers, declared himself for war, and from that day onwards there appeared the many obvious signs of a maritime nation preparing for war. Steamer sailings were cancelled or "postponed", and the mercantile fleet was recalled to home waters from all points of the compass. On the Sunday following the conference, while sailing in Kobe harbour, we saw men in bosun's chairs obliterating funnel markings

5

and ships' names and painting the funnels black and the hulls dark grey.

Soon came drastic internal censorship regulations and intense police supervision. One was permitted to speak only Japanese over the telephone; all letters sent through the mails were opened; police permits had to be secured by foreigners for even the shortest rail trips, and for all practical purposes foreigners, especially potential enemies, were interned in the places where they lived.

Eric and I made many plans for getting away in "Spray". We even laid in a stock of food and studied the route from Japan to Canada; we had complete confidence in our boat and would have gone to the ends of the earth in her. But all our plans came to grief over the same obstacle: to get out of Osaka Bay we had to pass through Kii Suido, a narrow channel only a mile or so wide. As this was one of the two major entrances to the Japanese Inland Sea, it was a very sensitive spot and had always been closely guarded by the Japanese Navy. In fact, to have come within thirty miles of it was an offence which would have landed us in gaol for years. It was quite impossible to get away from Japan in that way. However, my pestering of the British Consul at last bore fruit and, after two years, in the late summer of 1941, I secured a half-promise. I was to go to Singapore via Shanghai, Hong Kong and Manila, to work there in a civilian capacity. Enlistment in the Armed Forces, on which I had set my heart, was not promised definitely, but was held out as a possibility. The necessary travel arrangements were made, and I left Kobe after six years, in September 1941, on one of the last regular passenger steamers bound for Shanghai.

A few months earlier, Japan and Russia had concluded a pact of non-aggression. This had secured Japan's rear, of which she had always been fearful, and things were now moving rapidly until, by the time I left, her entry into the war had become a matter of weeks rather than of months—it was no longer a case of "if" but of "when". And still the Lotus Eaters refused to see what was in front of their eyes.

The complacency of some British officials in the Far East was not exactly encouraging, and when I got to Shanghai I heard many officers who should have known better, echo the same old chorus: "The Japanese won't start anything now, they know it would be suicide." That was at a time when Japanese transports were leaving in constant streams, day and night, bound for bases on Hainan and in French Indo-China, convenient springboards for attacks on Hong Kong and Malaya. Further, the Army had called up a million reservists in two instalments, and we all knew this.

But no one wanted to believe the facts that were under their noses. People who had never been to Japan, and who had never studied Japanese economics, politics or psychology, told me exactly what Japan was going to do and not do, when and how. The gist of American and British opinion in those twilight months before December 1941 was that, with Russia unbeaten on her doorstep, with China still kicking, with Britain undefeated and the United States gaining military power at a tremendous pace, Japan was likely to wait and see. In any case, she was said to have been exhausted by four years of war in China. Others pontificated that Japan would have to knuckle under quickly because she lacked oil and other raw materials which the democracies would not supply to her in case of war.

These were the unshakeable opinions of a majority of British and American residents in the Far East, and their convictions grew stronger as the weeks passed and nothing apparently happened. Right up to the first week in December an orgy of wishful thinking dictated the ostrich policy for which we were to pay dearly.

MANILA OCCUPIED

I was sitting at breakfast in Manila on 8th December 1941, when the news came through that the Japanese had started their war.

I had arrived some weeks earlier from Shanghai and had taken up quarters in the European Y.M.C.A. in Calle Concepcion because it was a quiet and unobtrusive place. It was intended that I should spend some time in Manila and then proceed to Singapore.

At first, on that fine tropical morning, we did not believe the news that Pearl Harbour had been bombed by the Japanese. There had been similar rumours flying about for weeks, and this might be just another one. But the newspaper arrived and confirmed the story with black headlines three inches high.

Some of us had known with certainty that it would come. And yet, despite all the evidence to the contrary, which we had had for months, it just did not seem credible that they had taken the plunge.

After breakfast I went downtown to draw some money from the bank and to hear more news. Driving into town I felt immediately a different atmosphere; the pace had quickened, cars travelled faster and sounded their horns more often. In Calle Escolta, Manila's fashionable shopping street, small groups of men discussed the news and shops boarded up their windows, concealing the gay Christmas displays. There was a great hustle and activity in the quarter around the Japanese bazaars, where trim and tough-looking Filipino soldiers from the Philippine Constabulary were rounding up Japanese shopkeepers and their assistants, and loading them into orange buses commandeered from the authorities, to take them off to internment. Japanese faces never betray much emotion, but I noticed that although some looked worried, the majority wore an arrogant grin.

We were back around noon at the Y. expecting an air-raid, and sure enough it came. Shortly after twelve-thirty twenty-seven silvery aeroplanes high up in the pale-blue sky flew over towards the naval base at Cavite, and Nichols Field aerodrome. Soon there came the dull rumbling of bombs, like cargo dropped in the hatch of a ship, and dark smoke rose from the bombed area.

That night under a tropical sky, which seemed far too bright in the strict blackout, I sat up for a long time on the broad verandah talking of the great topic of the day. With me was K. G. Stevens, an American businessman and technician, who represented a firm making some sort of wonderfully complicated American office machinery. We had chummed up since my arrival two months earlier and had gone on several trips and picnics together, and he had told me about his home in California and his business, and of the disregard with which the general public in America treated the Japanese threat. Now here we sat in Manila, waiting for the Japanese bombers to come back and add to the destruction of their noon raid.

Soon they flew over again, high above the arcs of yellow tracers that went up from the ground, and when they left, the city was red with fires.

On the following day and the day after, the Japanese repeated their bombing, flying in perfect formation and quite undisturbed by the ack-ack fire of our guns. We heard President Roosevelt's speech to Congress demanding the Declaration of War to the accompaniment of bombs dropping on Nichols Field.

Events now followed each other too quickly for us to follow them. The Japanese landed in strength in the north of Luzon; an attack south of Vigan was beaten off and the people were elated—until the Japanese attacked again the following day and succeeded. We had two false air-raid alarms, due to nervous Boy Scouts operating the sirens. They were replaced by the City Police—not that it made much difference, since the bombs usually dropped before the sirens went off. There were rumours that German pilots were manning the Japanese bombers—this was nonsense, of course, but people groped for any explanation of the uncanny accuracy of the bombing. Were not the Japanese all short-sighted? Surely the little yellow men couldn't do all this? People got cables from home with words of encouragement which sounded like sarcasm. One such read: "Give 'em both barrels," to which the receiver replied: "Send barrels."

Then there came over the Australian short-wave radio news that H.M.S. "Prince of Wales" and "Repulse" had been sunk from the air. What the Nazis had vainly tried to do for two years, the Japanese had succeeded in doing two days after the shooting started. Everyone was deeply depressed; the loss of two capital ships would almost certainly prevent reinforcements from being sent into Malaya and the Philippines before our outnumbered forces would be forced to fall back.

Again I got that feeling of being a trapped animal that I had known first in Germany, and later in Japan. I began to think of escape. My main object was to get a chance of fighting on reasonably even terms, that is, with a rifle in my hands. The fear of internment did not greatly worry me, many others had faced that, but I was a young man and I wanted to be in the fight.

Japanese troops now made further landings in force. On 20th December they went ashore 500 miles south of Manila at Davao, the capital of Mindanao where 18,000 Japanese civilians were living before the War. Another enemy force landed on Luzon well to the north near Damortes, and they had the west coast pretty well in hand as far south as the Lingayen Gulf.

Just before Christmas, the people under whose direction I worked told me what I already knew: that all normal communications had broken down and it was no longer possible for them to despatch me to Singapore. In any case, they had their own troubles there. Our Chief was lucky enough to be taken off by submarine, and the rest of us were advised to do the best we could and to make a getaway if we got the chance.

For many days now my mind had been fully made up that the Japanese would not get me for long, if at all. I was constantly thinking of ways and means to make a dash for it, and to get to free soil, preferably British, from where I could take up the fight with a sporting chance. I had sufficient confidence in my ability to fool the Japanese about my citizenship status and about my activities long enough to make a getaway. How grateful I was now that I could speak their language, which, a few months ago, I thought was a wasted asset. The first moments of contact would be the worst.

Basically my problem was one of timing. I knew that I could not hope to leave the city while every road leading to it was likely to be filled with oncoming Japanese, but I could not afford to leave it too late either. Immediately after their entry into Manila, the Japanese would begin the task of consolidating their position, and of regulating all civilian traffic. A system of passes and check points would be instituted throughout the country and this would make a getaway more difficult. There was nothing speculative about this, it had all been done before in China, Manchuria and everywhere else the Japanese went. My problem was, then, to try and time my departure to fit nicely between the Japanese occupation and consolidation of their positions in and around the city, and I had to check the impatience that now got hold of me.

Meanwhile I made paper plans and tried to convert what valuables I had to cash. My ultimate aim was, of course, a boat that I could sail single-handed or with anyone who would come along. Steve, and so many others who were not familiar with sailing, believed that almost anything was preferable to risking it in a small boat. I tried in vain to make them realize that size by itself did not matter, and that a boat of any given dimensions—as long as it complied with the minimum requirements of seaworthiness—was as safe as the "Queen Mary", if competently handled.

When I tried to talk people into giving it a go with me they smiled and thought I was crazy. They still thought that the American Fleet would come in any day and turn the tables or that, if they really were interned, it would be for a couple of months only. This wishful thinking was a sort of protective covering. Had they let themselves imagine the possibility of enduring hardships, indignities, torture and slow starvation for years, it might have been another story. I did not know of these things either then, but at least I had some inkling of how the Japanese went about their business, and I tried not to fool myself.

I saw the war in the Philippines and elsewhere in the Far East as, above all, a matter of distances. The Japanese were nearest, their lines of communication were intact and they had local air and naval superiority. On the other hand, the Allied fleets were fully occupied thousands of miles away, or partly immobilized. Our air forces just did not exist in this part of the world. One did not have to be a military genius to realize that it would be a long time before we could be rescued.

All I could do was to tell my friends what I thought, and beg them to try and escape with me. Men who had their families in Manila I did not ask, but those who were single, or whose families were overseas, I tried my best to persuade.

Meantime the bombing went on. There were air-raids now every day, but none at night after the 10th. There was no need for the Japanese to fear the daylight; aerial opposition over the city was almost nil. The few fighters left were fully occupied over the landing points. The Japanese made quite a mess of Cavite naval base, and of Nichols Field 'drome. There was also a good deal of bombing in the port area, but the city itself was left untouched at first.

We adjusted our lives to the new routine. It was surprising how monotonous air-raids could become. The first few days we ran for shelter every time the big planes with the "Fried Egg" markings appeared. But later we stood on the roof or in the streets and watched the pretty picture, unless the cargo started dropping too close for comfort.

During one raid we sheltered in one of the outworks of the Walled City, built by Chinese forced labour for the Spaniards in the sixteenth century. The thick, moss-covered walls with their low archways gave a feeling of security. And there were frangipani and other tropical flowers about, all smelling sweetly and looking pretty—an atmosphere out of tune with the scene of violence and destruction around us. Many Filipinos sheltered with us; they had defeat written all over their faces.

We had to be onlookers; we could not help and we had no means of fighting back—and the time was not yet ripe for a bid to escape. So we carried on with a travesty of the old social life because there was nothing else to do and in any event few of us were willing to believe the worst.

Christmas was a farce. On Christmas Eve I went to a cocktail party at the house of one of the newspaper men. It was so incongruous as to be almost comical; every few minutes the house shook as buildings and bridges went up, exploded by United States engineers, who had begun demolitions. Yet we drank and observed the ceremonial customary at cocktail parties—one of the more fatuous forms of entertainment. I tried to get a glow on, but it was no good; one must be in the mood to get drunk, and this wasn't the time.

I went to an uninspiring service on Christmas morning and lunched with a Dutch friend at the Manila Hotel. In the middle of the main course the bombs started, unannounced as usual, and we found ourselves gazing into each other's eyes underneath the table. Stevens and I had been asked to the Willimonts' for dinner, and we made an effort to preserve an appearance of the right spirit in front of the children. Packages wrapped in gaily coloured paper were exchanged and enjoyed by the smaller ones, but it was all a bit hollow.

On Boxing Day Manila was declared an Open City by General MacArthur to save the population from unnecessary hardship, and all guns were removed from the Luneta, the big square near the Manila Hotel.

As if to demonstrate their contempt for international law, the Japanese Air Force attacked the inner city for the first time on the following day. I was with Stevens half a mile off when it happened, and we saw the beautiful old Santa Domingo church on fire. This part of the Walled City was badly damaged, but the area was only three hundred yards from ships in the Pasig River, which were painted grey and were legitimate targets. They should have been moved earlier, but rumour had it that the Filipino crews had deserted. But then, there were so many rumours.

And so we watched the city die, bit by bit, as landmarks were destroyed and services disrupted. The homeless wandered desolately looking for their belongings among the rubble, the burned-out cars and the large craters that were everywhere.

As 1941 drew to a close, the fate of the city was no longer in doubt, and the Japanese bombers now turned their attention elsewhere. Corregidor, the mighty fortress guarding the entrance to Manila Bay, was raided, but it was not such an easy prey and three planes were shot down.

As if to seal the doom of Manila, the American Army engineers now set to work blowing up the Pandacan oil installation. This was a huge tank farm, and it burned for a week. Burning oil spilt into the Pasig River, which flowed through Manila, and the sack of Rome could not have looked more lurid than Manila at night. The fires were everywhere. Radio transmitters, telephone exchanges, the cold-storage plants, all were destroyed. Army barracks

from which the American and Filipino forces had withdrawn were set on fire. For nights the fires raged and
explosions from demolition charges shook the earth.
Large craters were blasted in the runways of Murphy and
Zablan airfields and their installations were wrecked. What
the Japanese Air Force had started, the Army engineers
finished, and New Year's Eve produced what must have
been one of the biggest New Year fireworks in history.

On New Year's Day 1942 we heard the final and rather
pathetic broadcast from a Government station, the last to be
destroyed: "God Save America, Keep 'em flying." The
telegraph stopped that afternoon. Only now was the full
truth of the situation dawning on many. We were cut off
completely from the outside world.

The suffering of the big city was almost over. The
military situation on the ground had become desperate. The
Japanese had now reached flat country north of Manila in
Nueva Ecija Province, out-flanking the Lingayen front still
held by the American Forces, and could deploy and use their
numerical superiority to the full. The United States Armed
Forces shortened their fronts north and south of Manila and
fell back towards the Bataan Peninsula. This meant that all
Luzon south of Manila, as well as the city itself, was abandoned.

The Japanese entered the City of Manila on 2nd January
1942. This was my diary entry for that day:

"The looting is terrible, the disarmed police powerless.
The Japanese are expected in the city this afternoon or
evening. Wish to get it over with quickly now. Saw
mobs break into Chinese groceries in the fashionable
Ermita district. Fires are everywhere. Saw bedlam near
the Post Office where the mob looted a small ship which
was already half ablaze. People snatched goods from the
burning hold—a fiendish sight. Sternberg military
hospital across the road from the Y. is dead since the army

15

moved on. American nurses used to work there and relax on the verandah after a hot day. Now the rabble of Manila is clearing the place of beds and of all that can be moved.

"Spent this morning watching the doomed and burning city from the roof of the tall building in which Steve has his office. The fires on the river, the Santiago forts, the piers and half a dozen other blazes in the Walled City make an unforgettable sight, and Steve takes pictures with his film camera. I wondered where he thought to have them processed, but did not ask.

"Saw the editor of the 'Manila Bulletin', I wish he would get out of the city. I was unable to get my idea across to him to publish an appeal that all car owners should destroy their vehicles, giving detailed instructions on how to do it. He agrees but says the idea that Mr. Jones should take the sledge hammer to his beautiful Packard is even now too alien to the possessive mind. I am furious, knowing from the Japanese record in China that all cars will be confiscated and used immediately against us. In any case, it would be too late now.

"While having a shower at the Y.M.C.A., at seven p.m. in the fading daylight, lorries full of Japanese soldiers drive through our street, Calle Concepcion. There are no people in the streets, no cheers, no jeers. They are here, and the curtain of lead comes down. All the nausea accumulated in recent years, while watching the rise of a nation infected with the diseases of aggression, intolerance and hate, wells up at the sight of the peaked caps with the yellow stars, and of the Japanese flags flying from every lorry. I will get away or go down in the attempt. I shall fight them another day.

"At nine p.m., a detachment came to the Y., and places us in confinement on the second floor. Guards are posted all over the place and the interpreter informs us politely that anyone trying to get out will be shot. He has a printed map of the city with him at which I looked. It was over-printed with Japanese characters. Their preparations were very thorough."

LAST DAYS IN MANILA

On the day following the Japanese entry into Manila some four hundred of us were interned in the Bay View Hotel, which normally accommodated a hundred and twenty guests. We were then given a preliminary examination by the Kempetai, the Japanese Military Police.

The guards locked all doors and windows, and the heat in the lounge where we had been dumped became oppressive. The guards continued to bring in more white men and women who had been picked up in their homes. No one was allowed in or out, and sentries were posted all over the place. The troops appeared to be fairly well seasoned and their peasant faces bore an implacable expression.

How well I knew those uniforms: the baggy, ill-fitting trousers and loose tunics with the red flash of the infantry; the peaked caps with the yellow star, looking ridiculously like undersized jockeys' caps on their bullet heads; putties wrapped untidily round their bandy legs in a manner which would have made any British sergeant-major wince. The Japanese Army never cared much for dress; in fact, smart dressing was looked upon as a form of affectation. These fellows were of the infantry all right. Much as we hated them, as fighters they always earned our respect. They never fought cleanly because they were never taught to, but physical courage in the attack and devotion to duty they had in plenty.

Soldier clerks, assisted by Filipino Quislings and informers, began taking down the personal particulars of new arrivals. I pitched them a yarn which I felt confident would do the trick and let me out eventually. The examination was as yet rather superficial, and I hoped to get away from Manila

17

before they had time for the more thorough check-up which was sure to come. The N.C.O.s were quite surprised to hear me answer their questions in Japanese.

An elderly Englishman and I did the interpreting. We tried in vain to make our captors release the head of the American Red Cross, who wanted to look after his patients and valuable Red Cross stores; but it was no use, the guards were very strict and would not even permit a patient with apoplexy to be transferred to a hospital. The comic relief was provided by an elderly American who was very agitated at having his hundred-and-fifty-dollar watch taken from him by a soldier. It was strange how the loss of property affected people differently; there were men there who had lost in a second the fruits of a lifetime's work and who seemed quite unconcerned.

The food position became grim. The Japanese did not provide anything, and we lived on the stocks of the hotel. We usually had one real meal a day, a plate of corned beef and potatoes, and there was still plenty of good American coffee. All the servants having left, the "guests" ran the hotel on a roster.

From an upper room we could see Dewey Boulevard, world-famous strutting place of dashing young Filipinos, dignified Americanos and Chinese baby amahs with their young charges, now occupied by Japanese soldiers trying to fix stalled and sabotaged cars. The Yacht Basin was deserted, the beautiful ships sunk or gone, a few masts sticking forlornly out of the water. Not a dinghy was afloat. The Pandacan tank farm was still ablaze and smoke rose from the direction of Corregidor and Bataan, where American Forces were still holding out.

For three days we just sat around in the stuffy hotel lounge and waited.

On 5th January I was let out of the Bay View Hotel together with the nationals of neutral countries. At the same time American, British and other Allied nationals were transferred to Santo Thomas University grounds, which had been set up as a permanent internment camp, and I had to say goodbye to Stevens. How I wished he could have come with me. There were many others whom I met again after the War, but I never saw Steve again.

My story of being a good German who had a small business in a provincial town south of Manila had worked so far. I was requested to report to the Military Police in the city to fill out forms and get passes. But now I was free, I had to live on my wits. The Japanese would be rapidly extending and tightening their grip on the life of the city, and I had to work against time if I wanted to get away.

First I moved all my belongings to the apartment of a Dutch friend. For this purpose I hired a couple of coromattas, the two-wheeler cabs drawn by scrawny ponies, which had again appeared in the streets. The Japanese Military Police ordered us to report weekly and forbade us to change our place of residence without their permission. But that was just the regulation to be ignored, and during the few days I remained in Manila, I slept almost every night in the house of a different acquaintance.

The city was a sorry sight. Life had been resumed again, after a fashion, and the people appeared relieved during these first days of the occupation. The known, however unpleasant, is always preferable to the uncertain. At least there were no raids now, and the Japanese had left them alive. They were happily ignorant as yet of the misery and oppression in store for them.

But the trouble was already beginning. In the city there were bread-lines, rice rationing was introduced and the black market was born. The price of rice had already doubled.

The Japanese had issued proclamations setting parity for their military currency with the Philippine pesos. That, of course, started a tremendous spurt of inflation, with the military currency being fed into the country as quickly as the printing-presses in Japan could run. In reality, it was a refined form of looting.

But there was old-fashioned looting as well. Although most shops had been closed and boarded up, Japanese parties broke into many of them. The Chinese had always been fair game for the Japanese and there was no checking the plunder in that direction. They concentrated on food stores. As the Chinese controlled almost all of the country's retail trades, dislocation set in at once. Stores and business premises owned by Americans and other Europeans, also banks, were sealed with a thick white paper label. One of the city newspapers came out again, but it was a sorry rag, Japanese propaganda from beginning to end.

The city's utilities were still not functioning and garbage was piling up in front of all the houses. A dreadful smell hung over the place. But the city fathers—wherever they were then—could hardly be blamed, since the Japanese had commandeered all forms of transport, especially trucks.

Apart from the looting of Chinese stores, there were few outrages reported within the city, but from the suburbs came reports of looting by small bands of soldiers guided by Japanese civilians. These people were a particular pest. They were residents with detailed local knowledge and could guide the soldiery to rich spoils. Fortunately, the Japanese troops left the liquor stores alone and few were drunk.

If there was rape, we never heard of it. White women were not molested. For that they could thank the fact that the Japanese ideal of feminine beauty is quite different from ours. They like their women small, with jet black hair and of an even olive complexion. In their eyes, white women have sharp pointed noses and white mottled skin. Later the Filipino girls were not so lucky.

Away from the city the War went on. The Japanese Air Force lost little time in making the airfields round the city ready for use, and after a few days planes were roaring to and from Nichols Field again.

Smoke rose continuously from Corregidor across the Bay, and from the Bataan Peninsula, but the stand there could be nothing more than a heroic rear-guard action. Even if more American troops had been handy at the time, the American fleet could not have risked sending them through narrow passages dominated by Japanese aircraft. The example of "Prince of Wales" and "Repulse" was too fresh.

Bataan and Corregidor did in fact hold out for three more months. They fought there one of the finest defensive campaigns in the history of war, led by that beloved officer, Lieutenant-General Jonathan Wainwright. While General MacArthur occupied himself with grand strategy in the concrete fastness of the Malinta tunnel and finally was ordered to Australia, "Skinny" Wainwright, in poor health and leaning heavily on his walking-stick, visited his troops in the front line. He stayed with them to the end and was interned on Formosa and later in Manchuria. He died in 1953, eight years after his release from captivity.

Later, the fame of this action was smothered by the well-publicized sweep of MacArthur's armies from New Guinea back to Tokyo, but the officers and men of the American and Philippine armies who lived to tell the tale had a special light in their eyes when they spoke of Wainwright. The name of General MacArthur did not evoke quite that sort of reaction. Maybe many of the things they said about him were cruel and unjust, nevertheless, troops have a fine nose for their commanders' strengths and weaknesses.

The Willimont family were among those British and American families who had been left in their homes when the first round-up for internment was made, and after I came out of the Bay View Hotel I had a long talk with my friend Willimont about my escape plans. He was all against my trying, but he could see that my mind was made up, and he was willing to help me.

I knew it could be done. It was being done every day from occupied countries in Europe. There, the Germans patrolled closely a coastline a couple of thousand miles long and still people were getting away from Norway, from Belgium, Holland and France. Coastlines in the Philippines were scores of thousands of miles long, and there were literally hundreds of islands on which the Japanese were unlikely to set foot for a long time yet. Further, we had heard that the large southern islands of Cebu, Panay and Mindanao were still in our hands.

From the city I wanted to go south to the west coast of Luzon, somewhere in Batangas Province, and over from there to Mindoro Island. There were no buses or trains functioning, so the first thing to do was to get a car.

As I had left it too late to draw out my remaining bank balance, I sold my expensive Leica camera outfit in a Filipino shop—and got a ridiculously low price for it. But at least I had some cash in my pocket now. I then walked to the Santo Thomas internment camp, where the guards permitted us to talk through the fence, and I was able to arrange for food and other supplies to be brought into the camp to some of my friends.

Through the fence I also arranged to buy the car of a Dutch friend for three hundred pesos and to pay the money to some relatives of his who were still free. The car was a 1935 Chevrolet two-seater, and it rather frightened me. Roads were poor and taxis cheap in Japan, so I had not driven for over six years and had never held a licence in my life. But someone showed me how to work the levers and pedals and I did a few trial runs without damaging anybody. The main thing was to know where the water and petrol had to go in; for the rest, I dared not look under the bonnet and I prayed that nothing would go wrong.

Since I planned to take only what I could carry, packing was not easy. I had to leave almost all my belongings behind. First I took all my private photographs out of their heavy albums and wrapped them in layers of oiled paper and an old piece of sailcloth. In my kit-bag I packed mostly clothing, khaki shirts and shorts, a spare pair of shoes, a pair of flannels, my favourite tweed jacket, a mosquito net, raincoat and pullover. Of my pipe collection I took the six I liked best. Everything else I left behind, including the curios I had collected in Japan, my beautiful Korean camphorwood chest, my Peking rug and all my books. Only the books really worried me; they were mainly on sailing in small ships, and were a collection it had taken me some time to get together. But it didn't really matter.

One of my acquaintances had Filipino relatives, who agreed to keep my belongings in safe custody, and did so for three years, until everything went up in flames when the Japanese razed the residential district of Manila during their retreat in 1944.

By 12th January my plans were as definite as they could be, and I decided to leave the next day. Willimont had given me a large road map of the islands, and I was going to try and reach the Batangas coast by making a considerable detour to the north and east of Lake Laguna. Since the main arteries feeding Manila from the south were on the west side of the lake, by avoiding them I hoped to miss most of the Japanese and, indeed, I got as far as Antipolo without any interference from the few soldiers who were guarding road crossings. It was the blown-up bridges that beat me. After Antipolo the road became impassable, and there was nothing for it but to turn back to Manila. I was in the city again by noon and now had no choice but to leave by one of the main roads running west of the lake.

Next morning, on 13th January, I surreptitiously filled up my tank with aviation petrol, which had been distributed by the United States Army before their stores were fired, and left Manila behind for good.

II. TO ILOILO

ESCAPE TO LOOC

ALTHOUGH one day's delay did not seriously upset my timing, there were many things that could still go wrong, and having to take one of the main south roads wasn't going to help me; so I was pretty anxious when I set out from Manila for the second time. But luck was with me. I was held up at guard posts only twice, on the outskirts of Manila and just before reaching Tuy, where a bridge had been blown up, and each time I got away with my story that I was a German "driving to my residence", which was always in a town a few miles farther on.

This invention was greatly helped by my "pass", which was, in fact, my commercial Power of Attorney, an imposing legal document of several pages complete with consular and duty stamps and coloured notarial seals. I held this out to the sentries with as much nonchalance as I could manage. They examined it from all sides with a great air of understanding, nodded knowingly as they handed it back to me, and were so much impressed that they did not examine the car. One zealous Private First Class did what he thought was the right thing and fingered me all over; he then lifted the bonnet of the car and searched under the seat, but he did not open the dicky-seat where my luggage was.

I had a much closer shave on a detour road skirting Lake Taal when the car bogged down by the rear axle in a sandy ridge, and near as a touch turned over into the lake. Fortunately deliverance was close at hand. Some farmers, who were ploughing near by with water buffaloes, hitched their beasts to the Chev. and pulled me out. Back on the main road I hardly saw a soul. There was no traffic of any kind, the towns along the Batangas coast were deserted and only a few sinister-looking Filipinos with their bolos, those long deadly Filipino knives, were at large.

That evening I reached Lemery, a small, almost deserted town on the sea coast, and there I found lodgings for the night in an unused bakery belonging to a Palestine Jew who called himself Mohammed Ali Moises—a rather unlikely mixture of fire and water, but it was not polite to comment. He pointed out the Chief of Police, who was lurking in the streets in civilian clothes—all the other officials and most of the townspeople had disappeared into the hills. I spoke to a few scared-looking people who were bemoaning their shot chickens and looted shops, but they knew little of what was going on and had not even heard that Manila had fallen a fortnight earlier.

The able-bodied men who had stayed behind were a gangster-like lot; I knew the faces by now. They were the same type which I had seen among the looters in Manila. When I approached them about a boat, they looked at me with long, calculating stares and I could feel them weighing the possible advantages of delivering me to the Japanese against falling in with my proposition that they should hire me a boat and take my car.

The situation began to be menacing. If I didn't get away quickly by sea, I could see my escape coming to an end almost before it had begun. But how was I to get a boat? I had already made every inquiry I could think of.

At this critical moment the Chief of Police decided to help me. He promised to get me a boat for Mindoro the next morning, after telling me that soldiers were patrolling the locality almost daily!

I spent an anxious night, and the next day the Chief of Police was as good as his word. He hired a banca for me—at an outrageous price. The banca was very small, no more than an outrigger canoe with a little sail, which could be paddled quite fast by her crew of two when the wind gave out. Before leaving, I hid my car in the back-yard of a fruit-shop after messing it up as well as I could. I had driven only sixty miles in it.

Early on the morning of 15th January we paddled away from Luzon Island making for Maricaban, a small island midway between Luzon and Mindoro, and arrived without incident. Maricaban was a pretty place with coconut plantations and small farms neatly fenced with bamboo spikes to keep out the inevitable pigs, and everywhere underfoot tough chickens pecked and squawked. Most important, there were about twenty schooners laid up there and my hopes rose. But the sailors were a tough-looking lot and the island people were full of suspicion, and I was making no headway at all until I discovered a man who could speak English. After that it was fairly easy. With his help I got a passage in an outrigger sloop, the "Gloria", due to sail at midnight.

I had just completed arrangements when another banca came in from Lemery and reported that about an hour after I had left, a Japanese patrol in two lorries had arrived there inquiring for a white man with a car. This didn't help me to wait patiently for midnight and I kept a keen look-out for Japanese pursuit from Lemery. But we got away safely.

I lay down with the brown crew on the hardwood planks, but my mind was too active for sleep, and watching the stars rise and hearing the swish of the water, as a steady night breeze from the mountains of Luzon drove us along easily, gave me a new feeling of confidence. If only I could get hold of a single-handed boat reasonably quickly there was more than an even chance that I could get safely to Singapore.

We reached the small village of Dulangan on Mindoro early in the morning and stepped out on to a beach overrun by lean black pigs. Again I was greeted with considerable

26

suspicion, but after the village officials had examined my old residential permit from Manila I was allowed to go on.

It took me two more hops to reach Calapan, a provincial capital on Mindoro, late in the afternoon; the first by dugout and laborious paddling, the second by banca. This hiring of small boats was becoming an expensive business and stiffened my resolution to get my own boat as soon as possible.

Calapan was a typical small town of the Philippines, with some 17,000 inhabitants, and the officials were very friendly for a change. I called on the provincial Governor, whom I found playing mahjong, on the Mayor and on the Chief of Police, who promised me a special pass and a truck to take me south the next day.

In those in-between days after the Philippine Government had ceased to function in the islands and before the Japanese took over completely the public servants were in a tough spot. They had to choose whether to give up their jobs or carry on under the Japanese. This choice was particularly difficult for the Chiefs of Police, who were, after the Mayors, the most important officials in the cities and towns. If they stayed at their posts they might be labelled collaborators; if they left and abandoned their careers—perhaps to hated rivals—who would thank them for it? How could they earn a living? Perhaps the Japanese had come for good. It must have looked like it to many—they had captured the country easily enough. All these considerations made life very difficult for the Chiefs of Police, and their doubts were reflected in their attitude to me. Some were genuinely friendly and helpful, others actively hostile. I could never be sure what I should meet at the next town.

I was now committed to make the next stage of my journey by cattle truck, along with some fifty natives going to their homes in the southern islands. Among them were many Visayan sailors from the Central Philippine islands who had been stranded in Manila, and a good sprinkling of gaol-birds released when the Filipino authorities had opened the gaols before the Japanese occupation. One elderly fellow with a pleasant face and a superior knowledge of English was pointed out to me as a murderer. He confessed frankly to this, adding, "but it was a political murder", as if that made the thing quite all right. He told me that he had been contesting a local election against another man who got away with a bit more fraud than he did and consequently won out. My frustrated friend became "very angry" and killed his opponent with a bolo, one of the more popular Filipino tools for mayhem. He got five years for manslaughter and had served three.

I thoroughly enjoyed the fifty-mile ride south to Bongabong on the Mindoro east coast. The country was very wild and tropical, quite different from the tame, almost suburban, countryside around Manila. In many places the jungle came down to the edge of the gravel road and pigs started up in panicky flight as the lorry roared past. The casualties of our rather wild drive were one little pig and one chicken killed.

At dusk we arrived at Bongabong, where the road ended, the Mayor, clad in light-blue pyjamas, received me courteously and, after examining my credentials by the light of a candle, invited me into his grass hut to share his dinner. The feast was delicious, except for the "tuba", that dreadful fermented reddish brew which I was continually being offered—the "palm wine" of romantic travel books—but my sleeping-quarters in a nipah-grass house were stuffy and filthy.

From Bongabong I had planned to get a boat across Tablas Strait to Panay, the next large island, whose capital, Iloilo, on the south coast, was my objective. I had heard that American troops were still in control at Iloilo and I hoped to get reliable Pacific war news there and find a suitable boat.

But the weather turned bad in the night, with strong

south-east winds and rain, and we were weatherbound all day. I tried to walk off my impatience along miles of palm-fringed beach under a torn and wind-swept sky. How "Spray" would have gloried in this weather. Looking across the water, I could almost see the little white ship running before it, securely snugged down, her sweet run leaving a clean wake. I must get to Iloilo and get my boat if it cost my last centavo; this travelling in short stages was too haphazard and expensive.

At last I could stand the waiting no longer; so together with some of the Visayans, including my murderer friend, I set out to walk twenty miles farther south to a coastal village from which a boat was due to sail the next day. Every mile of that hike through swamps and long-abandoned coconut groves was an achievement. In some places we passed large tracts of fertile soil where the inhabitants were few and indolent and appeared content with rather less than we should consider the barest necessities of life, and in others we had to hire carabaos, the ubiquitous water buffaloes, to get us across the deep and rapidly flowing rivers. They weren't at all easy to ride. The native driver sat in front and one had to hang on astern like grim death, swaying to and fro, one's face continually fanned by a wet and dirty tail. However, we all got through, and we stumbled at last into the village after midnight—to find the boat gone. I was too exhausted to care about where I slept and gratefully shared a grass hut for the night with the owner's precious fighting cock.

Next morning, with what seemed incredible good luck, I got a passage on a cargo "Lorcha", a sixty-foot sailing-boat with a two-masted fore-and-aft rig, which was going to Tablas Island to the north of Panay. I have never seen such a collection of strings and patchwork sails; the standing rigging was equally moth-eaten and there were a few missing topside planks to give added interest. We had the wind well ahead of the beam most of the time, and when this queen of

29

the waves put her fat head into it, which was often, she not only stopped dead but water poured in through the gaps in her planking by the bucketful. Seldom had I seen such an ungainly swine of a boat. And I wasn't quite so sure of my luck when I was seasick for well over an hour. I had sailed on several of the seven seas in boats large and small in every weather, and this was the second time I had been sick. The first occasion was when I crossed the English Channel from Flushing to Harwich, where the same confused swells and hollow seas prevailed as here in Tablas Strait.

To add insult to injury, some nimble-fingered gentleman stole my best pipe, and this only a few days after my prismatic binoculars had vanished from the hut at Bongabong— probably the work of one of my gaol-bird companions. But everything ends, and so did this trip across Tablas Strait.

After arriving at Looc, the main town on Tablas Island, my usual battle with Filipino officialdom began again. This time I was put under arrest.

Not knowing who was in power or where, the police decided I was either one or all of the following: a Japanese spy, a Fifth Columnist, a German agent, an American officer in disguise, an American deserter or an English pilot. What I really was and what my credentials showed me to be, a refugee of uncertain status but of no uncertain allegiance, no one was inclined to believe.

I asked the zealous Chief of Police to get in touch with the American or Filipino authorities still operating on Cebu or Panay in order to get permission from them to let me pass. He agreed to do this, but took sensible precautions in the meantime, and I had my first experience of the inside of a stuffy and bug-infested police cell. With concrete walls, and one-inch bars on the doors, it was quite escape-proof, and I was kept there for two days until word came that I might be allowed to go to Panay.

To make amends and show that there was no ill feeling between us, the Chief of Police now had me quartered in the best room at the Municipio, the local-government offices, and shared his table with me, and while I waited for a passage to Panay we went rifle and revolver shooting in the hills together.

SANTA BARBARA AND ILOILO

Much against my will, I spent the next four months on Panay Island, the largest in the central Philippines, and for the first six weeks I was in gaol again.

When I arrived at Capiz the officials there, like those at Looc, decided immediately that I must be a dangerous person and sent me forthwith to the barracks of a Filipino Constabulary platoon at Santa Barbara, where they refused my request to contact someone in authority at Iloilo to take up my case.

For six weeks I was alone. There was nothing to read and no one to talk to. My food was sent up to me, my gaolers were polite but distant. Such snatches of news as I could get hold of were not calculated to help my morale: Singapore had fallen, then Java, and now the nearest free country was Australia, some three thousand miles away.

At this distance in time I can well understand the predicament of the police. With the infiltration by Japanese agents who had come to spy out the land, a man without a valid passport must have raised all their suspicions. But at the time I was in no state of mind to be judicial. I fretted and fumed; I counted every coconut on the few trees outside my window; I lost my sense of humour and my sense of proportion; but one thing I never lost, my will to get out.

Finally someone in Iloilo must have got to hear about me, because, one day in March, I was told that I could be off. To celebrate, I had a chicken dinner with the commander of the platoon, who had been my gaoler, we drank tuba together, and the next day an American staff car came to collect me.

But I wasn't exactly free. Although Panay was not yet

occupied, the Japanese had strategic command of the entire Philippine Archipelago, and it was only a question of time before they would garrison all the main centres.

For the present, the island was still under American and Filipino administration, but it was difficult to find out who was really in control. Most of the officials had taken to the hills and, since the central Government in Manila had ceased to function and the Japanese were still in process of setting up a puppet government, those who were left were uncertain of their authority.

The military organization was likewise rather puzzling. It was fairly obvious that Iloilo would not be defended. The city lay in a coastal plain without any of the natural obstacles which could have formed the backbone of a determined defence by a small force. Further, no attempt to prepare defensive positions had been made in or around the city, and all that stood between the citizens and the Japanese was a small delaying force of the Philippine Army under native officers.

So far, the performance of the Philippine Army could hardly inspire anyone with confidence. To be fair, the men were mainly raw levies, hastily called up and poorly trained. Man for man they were good soldier material; they were healthy, intelligent, willing to learn; they genuinely loved their country and they had a good cause to fight for. Whenever they were led by American officers, or by Filipino officers trained in the United States, the fighting record of Filipino troops was first rate. But the Filipino Officer Corps was pathetic—it could hardly be otherwise when wealth and family were the chief qualifications for a lieutenant's bars. These men knew all their privileges, they were magnificently turned out, but they had little sense of duty and responsibility. There were exceptions, of course, but the average Filipino officer with whom I came into contact was a swaggering gutless bully.

I had just had a good chance of observing the way the

Captain in charge of the platoon of Constabulary (a part of the Army) which had been guarding me at Santa Barbara administered his command. His N.C.O. would line up the men once a day and put them through a bit of ragged rifle drill, that was all. Never, during the whole six weeks, did I see the Captain carry out or supervise any training; he spent most of his time in his quarters sleeping, reading or drinking. As I had met many others like him, I wasn't counting on a spirited defence of Iloilo.

The city was already half deserted when I arrived, and all the hotels appeared to be shut and boarded up. Finally, I got a room at the only hotel still open, the Cosmos, a place of unsavoury reputation. It was really a bug-infested doss-house with no service of any kind, but at least the showers worked and I had a room to myself.

Iloilo must have been an enchanting place in normal days, and even now it had a gracious charm. It was the centre of the sugar industry, one of the most important industries in the Philippine economy. In the surrounding district the cane was milled and the raw sugar bagged for shipping, and down at the docks stood the large warehouses now stacked to the roof with mountains of bagged raw sugar.

The wealth from the sugar trade was reflected in the commodious bungalows, surrounded by large gardens ablaze with bougainvillæ and other tropical flowers. But the shutters were up now and the owners had fled to the hills; weeds were already springing up in the pathways, and the wide streets were empty save for an occasional sleepy patrol of Filipino soldiers in their blue dungarees.

The centre of the town had one or two business streets, where the most conspicuous feature was the number of name-plates of solicitors and barristers—a reflection of every educated Filipino boy's ambition. The Japanese offices and shops were shut and their owners interned, but the Chinese still did a roaring trade, and it was surprising to see how many imported goods were still available. Inflation had

33

already started, and prices were sky-rocketing by the hour.

The harbour was small and pretty. The Iloilo River flowed through the city and widened out before entering the sea, forming a natural anchorage with a narrow entrance protected by breakwaters. There was enough berthing space for five or six ocean-going vessels in the sugar trade and dotted about were many sailing-ships of all sizes, mostly schooners, great apple-cheeked double-ended things of stout build, and heavily sparred—any one of them would do the trip to Australia.

I particularly coveted a pretty little ketch painted white. She was about thirty-five feet over all and had a bold sheer and high freeboard. She was double-ended with the sharp stern commonly seen in these waters, and similar to a type of fishing-boat found in England and Scandinavia. Her spars were well proportioned, with a gaff mains'l and a thimble-headed mizzen, and she looked ideal for my purpose. But she wasn't mine, and I didn't see how I could get her. I hadn't enough money left to buy a boat, but I had to get one somehow. That had been my ultimate objective ever since I left Manila, and it was never out of my mind. But first, I decided to offer myself to the American authorities. If they were going to make a stand I reckoned they would want to use every able-bodied man.

As soon as I arrived in Iloilo, after dumping my gear at the Cosmos Hotel, I had gone in search of the British Consul. I found Mr. Lee a very nice man, but he was as isolated as the rest of us and couldn't help much. So then I went looking for the most senior American officer I could find; this was Colonel MacLaren, who held the posting of Port Quartermaster. I put two questions to him: could he enlist me or use me in any way? If not, what were the chances of my getting southward transport?

I didn't get far with an answer to either question. Like the British Consul, Colonel MacLaren was pleasant but noncommittal; however, he promised to write to headquarters, which was now situated in the mountainous central part of Panay, where a redoubt of strength had been prepared, and was commanded by an American, Major-General Christie.

I pestered Colonel MacLaren as I had pestered the British Consul in Japan, but it was some time before he received a reply, and meanwhile I got terribly impatient and bored.

I didn't know anyone in the town and I used to dine off a hamburger steak in a little joint across the street from the hotel and go back to my room every night. I read the few magazines lying around from cover to cover, and somebody lent me "Flowering Wilderness" which had always been one of my favourites—I had practically grown up on Galsworthy in a German translation. And while I read, the cicadas sang outside in the still air and the harsh call of the ghekko—the little buff-coloured lizard of the Philippines—would now and then break in on the silence of the room. The heat was stifling in the dry season, but I dared not undress because of the mosquitoes. They were a nasty kind, small and quick, and their sting hurt considerably; and they were difficult to catch, unlike the larger and more placid ones in Japan. Under the mosquito net at night the heat was terrible.

Although I was bored and frustrated, there were compensations. The beauty and insouciance of the tropics never failed to delight me. I found the cloud shapes and colours at sunset a singing glory, and I loved the brief twilight between light and dark when the vivid colours of earth and sky took on an added intensity. Often at night I would stroll down to the harbour through a coconut grove and look up at the slender and graceful palms silhouetted against the moon. The scented air was cool after the heat of the day, and there was silver on the sheet of water that was the great good sea.

Moored to the jetty, stout trading schooners stuck their heavy spars straight into the stars, their standing rigging taut, the ratlins weaving a delicate pattern through the shrouds. I would rejoice in the heavy dead-eyes and lanyards, reassuring signs that the sailing-ship tradition was not quite dead.

Then I went down with the fever. First I was delirious and after that I did not care very much what happened. A Filipino photographer who was staying at the Cosmos hunted up three small packets of tea for me and they were great medicine and revived me wonderfully. In the absence of drugs tea, when I could get it, was always medicine throughout this time, and I appreciated it as I had never done before.

Fortunately I was soon well again, but still there was nothing to do, and I was so bored I used to play patience. In my ignorance I thought the Americans would welcome with open arms anyone reasonably intelligent and strong who was willing to take up any job that needed doing, and each day I expected to hear from them. All the same, I couldn't keep my mind off buying a boat—but for that I had no money.

During this time there was little news, and what there was was bad. General MacArthur had gone to Australia to take up his new command, and reports came through that Japanese convoys were steaming towards the Australian mainland. In Burma, Britain did not seem to be doing well. Of the war in Europe, we heard nothing at all.

In my idleness and frustration I wrote furiously: diary entries about politics, about the War, the Philippines and whatever else came into my head, and I wrote love letters to my fiancée which could, of course, no longer be posted. Two years before I had become engaged to a Canadian girl who was teaching at the Canadian Academy in Kobe, the school for the children of the English-speaking foreign community. In Japan, the proportion of marriageable white girls to rapacious and prowling bachelors had been roughly one to twenty. It had been quite a feat to win her affection, and I was wildly and unreasonably in love for the first time. Early in 1941 she had been evacuated to Australia, and this was yet another reason—a powerful one—for me to get there as quickly as I could.

All these letters and diary scribblings killed some time, but I still wasn't getting anywhere, and complications set in. My personal papers and passes, which should have been given back to me by the Philippine Constabulary after my release from gaol, now appeared to have been lost, and I made many fruitless trips back to Santa Barbara where the reply was always the same: "mañana" they would turn up and be returned to me. These papers were important, they consisted of alien registration certificates from Japan and the Philippines, police clearances and similar travelling and identification records and passes.

Then more war news began to come through. One day the Japanese landed a small party on neighbouring Cebu Island, apparently for reconnaissance. A few days later they landed again and in strength, and also at Dumarguete on the south-east coast of Negros. With both Cebu and Negros, the large islands to the east and south of Panay, in the enemy's hands, the beaters were getting closer.

By now more than half the population of Iloilo had evacuated to the hills or to small neighbouring islands, and those who were left were grappling with the same situations and problems which had arisen in Manila three months previously, and in much the same way. There was the same deplorable lack of imagination, especially among the white community. It was like seeing a poor show at the circus for the second time in the same week. I knew all the acts; I had heard all the wishful thinking before, all the talk about reinforcements coming any moment. They were playing the same game of make-believe in Iloilo as had been played in Shanghai and Manila, and I was furious that I could do nothing. I continued to pester Colonel MacLaren, feeling every day more like a salesman trying to promote

37

some obscure make of vacuum cleaner in an overtraded market.

Each day a Japanese reconnaissance plane came over. He was only a little fellow high in the blue tropical sky, and we could just make out the red circle under his wing. No doubt he watched us extending the airfields with satisfaction. That would spare him extra work when the time came. Round and round he would drone in lazy circles for twenty minutes or so. He was quite contemptuous of us—anyway, we had nothing which would shoot high enough to touch him.

Meanwhile people went to the office at eight and came home at five, changed, and then had drinks, billiards and dinner. I don't think I had the wind up any more than the others, but I just could not see this stiff-upper-lip attitude as a courageous acceptance of the inevitable. We ought to have dug defensive positions, prepared road blocks and alternative positions in the hills. But nothing was done. There was an air of decadence and defeat about the place.

I tried to be patient; but patience is not always a virtue, of that I was sure, and my own need for action began to make me feel desperate. I began to feel trapped again—and still there was no word from the hills.

Food became dearer, and my funds were running out fast. I had a restaurant meal once a day, and for the rest ate melons, papayas, mangoes and bananas, which remained incredibly cheap right to the end. It was always a mystery to me why canned foods were so sought after both by the natives and the resident foreigners, when everything that came out of a tin was stale compared to the fresh food obtainable. It was really a form of snobbery. Those natives who could afford to buy a tin of tasteless Japanese canned pilchards looked down on their poorer neighbours who had to be content with fresh fish caught the same morning.

It was now late March, and my lack of money was

becoming desperate. I went to the local branch of the
Chartered Bank to try and draw against my Manila account
or raise a loan against my credentials. But my cheque book
said Manila instead of Iloilo, so I could not get my money.
It was rather absurd in the circumstances. Property worth
millions of dollars had already been destroyed in the islands
and the Japanese were on our doorstep—but still the books
of a small isolated bank branch had to balance.

After that came the unkindest cut of all. While I was
asleep, my wallet, containing what little cash I had left,
some papers and a photo of my girl, was stolen out of my
trouser pocket. The police got on to the job, but it was
hopeless from the start. I now had fourteen pesos and seven
centavos left in small change, there had been no word from
the Americans, and I could see no prospect of getting a boat.
I had reached rock bottom.

Then, miraculously, things began to improve. The
following day, when I went to see Colonel MacLaren, he
had an answer for me at last. No, they couldn't enlist me;
if I had been a Pole or a Dutchman it would have been
different, but I had no valid passport and had been born in
Germany, and that was the end of it. But he did have a
practical proposal. How would I like to work with the
military branch administering enemy alien property? A
great many Japanese shops and bazaars, also some German
properties, had been taken over when their owners were
interned at the outbreak of war, and the idea was to liquidate
these assets and deposit the proceeds with the banks still
operating, for settlement after the War against Allied properties taken or destroyed by the Japanese and Germans. It
was a ridiculous job, but I needed money, and it was something to do for the time being.

If I had been enlisted, that would have been the end of my
plans for getting a boat. But having been given a civilian
job instead, my determination to go south was renewed,
my papers "mislaid" at Santa Barbara, had now been

returned to me by the United States authorities, and to get away as quickly as I could became my constant preoccupation.

There was still a fairly large foreign community left in Iloilo, and I decided to try and organize an escape party to Australia. The first men I put the idea to were Verney and Leany, two mining engineers from one of the islands to the north of Panay, who were working with me on this job. But they would have none of it, and treated me as though I was a lunatic whenever I tried to persuade them.

In spite of this, we got along well. They had established themselves very comfortably with two Chinese houseboys in the bungalow of a wealthy gentleman who had evacuated, and invited me to join their mess. After four miserable weeks at the Cosmos I was delighted to accept.

Verney and Leany had lost all their belongings and arrived at Iloilo with what they could carry, and they told a sorry tale of what had happened on Masbate—their station— shortly before and after the Japanese got there. The Constabulary soldiers were the first to take to the hills, leaving their rifles neatly stacked in racks, and it was the same story as in Manila: looting by the Filipinos, hair-breadth escapes, and indecision concerning demolitions and defence. At first the Japanese had sent what was apparently a reconnaissance party of some fifty men in a single boat. They had left unmolested but returned a few days later in force, getting twenty thousand tons of precious fuel oil, which had not been destroyed, and much valuable mining equipment.

Together, the three of us had a lot of fun on our job as enemy property custodians. We even had to take stock, and spent several days counting Japanese paper hats, pocket knives, belts and other assorted merchandise. With the rest of the Pacific world in chaos, our occupation was more than ordinarily pointless. Nevertheless, we got a useful car out of it, a good laugh now and then and received salaries for our pains.

We spent the evenings at the Iloilo Club, a comfortable little bungalow right beside the beach and looking through palm-trees across Iloilo Strait to Guimaras Island, green and mountainous. A couple of servants were still left, and both the billiard table and bar functioned. It was good to have agreeable company again, even if the chief topic of discussion was often the dwindling stock of whisky.

But there were some of us with a great deal on our minds. There were Englishmen who had sent their wives and children to the islands or to the hills, and were greatly worried whether to keep them there or let them return and wait resignedly for the Japanese to come. During the two years before Japan came into the War the British authorities had advised their nationals to leave Japan, China and other Far Eastern areas and had even paid the fares where necessary, but some of the women had refused to leave their husbands, and now their plight was desperate.

Around the first week in April, the pace began to quicken and there was a feeling of impending action in the air. Even if we had had no other news, the behaviour of the Chinese storekeepers was a reliable indication. With their sixth sense for scenting trouble, they started boarding up their shops until it became almost impossible to buy anything. The price of cigarettes, soap, canned milk and other important goods went sky-high. A packet of "Lucky Strikes" sold for five pesos, or two dollars fifty in American currency. I was glad I smoked a pipe, which would burn almost anything.

At the Club and in the mess we made plans for escape, which all came to nothing. One idea was that a syndicate should buy from its Spanish owner the ketch which I had seen on my first day in Iloilo. But nobody put much heart into the scheme, and on my own I didn't have a chance in the world of raising the necessary three thousand pesos. Then I learned by chance that a Captain Herndon, an American yachtsman, who had sailed his boat from Singapore to

Manila the previous year, was fitting out right here at Iloilo for a dash to Australia. My heart leaped, I rang him up and asked for an interview. A smooth voice replied: "I know who you are, you're wearing khaki shorts, aren't you? Sorry to be so blunt, but there's no chance. I'm too busy to make an appointment to give you advice, but good luck to you."

Later I discovered Captain Herndon's ship in dock and I watched her on a trial spin in the sunny harbour. She was a strong cutter-rigged double-ender about forty-five feet in length. Her rig was quaint and the above-deck features even more so, notably a considerable house forward. The mast was rather tall, and the boom very high above deck; gaff also rather oversized and peaked medium-high. Not exactly a well-proportioned ship, but she looked strong and sound, and would probably take a lot of beating. She appeared slightly under-canvased.

From another side I heard that the boat was well found and had an engine which drove her along at a good clip. She was said to be well equipped with everything necessary: charts, navigation instruments and a large stock of food. Captain Herndon was sailing with his young wife and a native crew. I wrote to him applying for a job on board, but he never replied.

All the next day I watched him stow and make ready from across the basin. I had just enough pride left not to go over and try to speak to him. Usually yachtsmen weren't quite like him.

Looking out to sea, I could almost see my own boat "Spray" moored in one of the snug harbours in the Inland Sea of Japan, her white and shapely hull riding gracefully to her anchor—the Northill type which held well when it blew. She would have two stern lines out to the breakwater of rough boulders to prevent her shifting with the tides. Her coiled-up running rigging of soft cotton and Plymouth rope, the white sail well tucked in between boom and gaff in approved fashion . . . It was all before me. The awning would be over the cockpit to guard against the dew and my brother would be making tea in the snug cabin below—being the younger, he was usually landed with the galley. What a home she was, and how we loved her. We treated her well and knew her down to the last cleat, specially cast for us after a Merriman mould.

But what had happened to "Spray" and where was Eric now? I had heard nothing from him since December just before the bombing of Manila, and I greatly feared that he had been stranded in Japan.

Another plan came much closer to realization. It was around 10th April, at the same time as the Japanese announced over the Cebu wireless that they would land on Panay and occupy Iloilo the following week, that I discovered that an American naval officer, a four-striper full Captain, was fitting out a deep-sea fishing-boat which had been confiscated from some local Japanese fishermen. She was one of those ungainly ships, about seventy-five feet long, which one met everywhere in the Far East and in which the apanese had carried out much of their subversive activities under the cover of "fishing". She had a simple semi-diesel Bolinders engine and fuel for three thousand miles. There were over two hundred gallons of water, and provisions, already on board. The Captain and his two Lieutenants said I could come along as crew, it was as simple as that. They were going to try for Australia. My joy was boundless, and on 13th April I put my gear on board. We were to sail that afternoon.

The let-down was not long in coming. I waited for three hours in vain, and later that evening was told by someone from the Harbour Master's Office that the four-striper and his Lieutenants were to be flown to Australia. Strangely enough, I was not too disappointed; the scheme had been too good to be true. The next day I took my belongings off the ship again and helped myself to some of the provisions which had been left on board. I could never have managed this huge and ungainly thing on my own, and I didn't like boats with engines, anyway. Too much could go wrong, and they made such a hellish noise.

Shortly after this disappointment the SS. "Hai Kwang" came into Iloilo harbour. She was a small Yangtse River oil tanker belonging to one of the subsidiaries of Shell. The Captain and the First Officer were Englishmen, the Second Officer was a White Russian from Shanghai and the Engineer a Dane. They were all a bit weary and had had enough of it, except Skerr, the Mate. He was a comfortable Northumbrian with an inexhaustible supply of stories.

Theirs was a tale of close shaves. After leaving the China coast the previous October, the ship had been used to supply the American and Filipino garrison on Corregidor and Mariveles at the entrance to Manila Bay. They ran the Japanese blockade a couple of times and finally managed to get as far as Iloilo. They told us about the heroic stand at Bataan, and feared it would not last much longer. Food and ammunition were giving out and the Japanese had sunk most of the ships trying to bring food from the islands still in our hands.

Naturally, I tried to interest Captain Thistlewaite and his officers in a dash to the south. The "Hai Kwang" itself was out; they were unloading her, ready for scuttling, there was no other way, as they had only twelve days' bunkers and most of the native crew had deserted. My idea was to fit out one of the lifeboats, but the officers felt that they had ridden their luck hard enough, and they refused to come in on it.

Everywhere I encountered the same aversion to a small-boat voyage as I had met before in Manila. The "Hai Kwang" officers looked upon all yachtsmen with the distaste of the professional for the amateur, and the R.N.V.R., particularly the outfit formerly stationed at Hong Kong, was their pet aversion. I doubted whether they really meant it.

There was a lot of eat, drink and be merry these last days, and who could blame them? There were still four hundred bottles of "White Label" to be done away with.

When it became clear that nobody wanted to come with me and that they preferred to be interned, I asked Captain Thistlewaite whether he would give me one of his lifeboats. As a last hope, I thought I could go to some small leeward port and try to fit her out for sea. Both Captain Thistlewaite and the Port Captain gave their permission, and I started putting stores aboard her. This was on 15th April. I secured some maps and took the boat's compass from the other lifeboat as well. My lifeboat was far from ideal, but at least it would get me out of Iloilo, and after so many set-backs I was both excited and relieved at this eleventh-hour chance of escape by sea. I would be off within a day or two.

All that day, 15th April, the city emptied itself. There wasn't exactly panic, but the population was jittery. It had been much like this in Manila, and I, who prided myself on being clear-sighted, behaved as stupidly as everyone else in our small white community. Instead of getting the lifeboat ready for sea with all speed, I carried on half-heartedly with my futile job as enemy alien custodian and drank and played snooker with the others in the Club after work.

At 6 p.m. Father Kerr from the Augustinian College near by called at our mess and told us that landings had taken place on Panay, and I still didn't wake up to the immediate danger. There had been so many false alarms these last few days that we paid little attention to his news and went to bed.

That night, there was heavy traffic, and when we woke next morning at six o'clock, civilians were streaming out of the city along the road past our bungalow. But there were no detonations or fires to show that things were in earnest. Trains whistled as usual, and we thought that all was well. Then we discovered that there was no water in the taps, the electricity was off and the telephone dead. We had been caught unprepared again.

To Iloilo

It was now seven o'clock. I packed in great haste, and was just putting my gear in to the car when we heard the first explosions. Fires began to crackle, and machine-gun stutter came across the river. I raced through the burning town down to the harbour. Not a soul was in sight. There the "Hai Kwang" sat, but she was deserted and nobody answered my hail. She had not been scuttled. I tried to lower my lifeboat. I might have spared myself the trouble, it was quite impossible. Then machine-gun fire came from very close quarters, but I could not see from where. I became afraid and raced back to the car, forgetting even to take out the charts and compasses which I had stowed in the lifeboat. Quite irrelevantly, I noticed how sweet the frangipani smelt when I passed the little plantation in front of the Customs House. The door was open and I jumped out of the car and ran into one of the offices, but there was nobody there. I grabbed a book, "The Philippine Pilot", Volume I, but did not have the nerve to stay longer and look for some more useful reference books or charts. I was thoroughly frightened by now. There was much noise from fires and small-arms fire, but nobody was to be seen. That was strangest of all. I drove the car back through town to our bungalow without realizing that I had a flat tyre.

There were only two main motor roads leading out of Iloilo, and one of them was impassable because a bridge had been blown. The other ran along the south coast, and it was a certainty that the Japanese would be advancing along that route. There was no way out by car, so I took my gear back into the bungalow, and drove the car into a tidal flat near by, where she would be nearly covered with water at high tide.

There was nothing I could do now but wait on events and take any chance that came. I went back to the bungalow, and the three of us watched from there all day.

I remember it was a hot morning with white clouds sailing above and a stiff north-west breeze rustling the palms in the garden, while the town went up in flames and the buckling and rending of corrugated-iron roofing made a peculiar noise that sounded like shots.

Around ten o'clock in the morning the machine-gun and rifle fire stopped and we saw Japanese infantry on the other side of the river, advancing in deployed formation towards the main road leading from Jaro to Iloilo. Planes were continuously overhead, and we could see them letting down for landings on the fields we had just finished for them, which were quite undamaged. There was looting in neighbouring houses, and our Chinese boys were extremely frightened. They were not the only ones. And when, in the early afternoon, Father Kerr came across and suggested that we spend the next night in the Augustinian College, we accepted the kind invitation gladly.

LAST DAYS IN ILOILO

Compared to what happened at Iloilo, the occupation of Manila in January had been orderly and civilized. The troops who had been sent to Panay were a savage lot. They had originally taken part in the assault on Singapore, where they had lost heavily. Here, in the Visayas, they met with little or no opposition. They were on a detached command and behaved brutally.

When the Japanese entered Iloilo they found the residential and business districts almost completely gutted by fire, which deprived them of loot. This heightened their fury, and Filipinos were shot on the flimsiest pretexts and cruel revenge was taken for every act of sabotage, such as the frequent destruction of the water-pipes which led from the reservoir at Ma-Asin to the city. There was rape, and there was torture. In the suburb of Jaro, to the north of the city, the Japanese Captain of Military Police in charge instituted a rule of terror. Near the old Iloilo gaol I had to witness the torture and death of a young Filipino accused of he knew

47

not what. He was clubbed and kicked, went down and was jerked up again and again, until it was over.

Japanese soldiers looted that part of the town left standing, and were ably assisted in this by several hundred Japanese civilians now released from internment.

The pity of the burning was that objectives of military value, such as the dockyard, the railway sheds and oil installations, fell into Japanese hands undamaged. The Filipino unit in charge of demolitions was caught napping and vanished into thin air. Only business and residential districts on the right bank of the river went up in flames, and the stench of dead dogs and cats, mixed with the smoky smell of thousands of bags of sugar, hung for days over this once-sleepy tropical city. The sugar, turned to molasses, smouldered endlessly. All the Japanese properties of which we, as property custodians, had taken such meticulous inventory went up too, thanks be, together with all the books. So also did the Chartered Bank, which had refused to let me draw any money only a few days before; the whole place was destroyed, books, cash and all. A heap of rubble indicated the place where the Iloilo Club had stood, but at least the members had set to with hammers and destroyed the remaining 400 bottles of "White Label" before the Japanese got there. Symbolically, this was the only preparation which some made before they went into captivity —many of them, to death.

Many Spaniards and Filipino citizens with Spanish blood welcomed the Japanese. This seemed strange to me, but the same thing had happened in Manila. Technically, the Spaniards were neutral but, in fact, the Spanish population of the Philippines were by and large anti-American and gloated over America's defeat.

Wherever the Japanese patrolled outlying districts, a Spanish or Mestizo-Spanish Quisling would usually be there to guide them. It was understandable I suppose. Spaniards had been at the receiving end of their wars with Anglo-

Saxon people during the past few hundred years and now, pro-Franco almost to a man, I saw and heard many give detailed information to Japanese officers about the location of American property and military establishments. There were, of course, honourable exceptions, men who remained true to the flag of the Philippine Commonwealth, which had given to most of them their bread, and to many, a fortune.

The performance of the Philippine Army was a disgrace. Although the strategic position of the islands was hopeless from the start, and the superiority of Japan's well-trained troops, both in numbers and equipment, was smothering, nevertheless, throughout the Archipelago there were many natural features which offered good ground for prolonged resistance by determined and well-led troops.

When the Japanese arrived, the delaying force under native officers, which was stationed in and around the city, disintegrated without firing a shot. This was not just an isolated instance; the pattern was everywhere the same. At the mere mention of the word "landing" the troops would disappear and their officers were nowhere to be found, and when they told you about their part in the campaign afterwards, it was always the same: their platoon or company had been "disbanded" shortly after the Japanese landed. During the days before and immediately after the occupation of Iloilo, soldiers came to us asking quite unashamedly, "Say, Mister, have you got a spare civilian suit I could borrow?"

I remember Major X. the magnificent. He had been the Intelligence Officer and cut quite a dashing figure. His work, whatever it was, had been so terribly secret that he had INTELLIGENCE embossed in gold-lettering on his brief-case. He talked big then about a last-ditch stand in the hills, or of escaping with me to Australia. He looked every inch the American Regular, with knife-sharp creases in his khaki trousers, and immaculately ironed shirts.

By chance I ran into this hero some weeks later in a small

49

hamlet in the mountains of a small island. There he sat, without gold leaves of his Major's rank, a small and rather pathetic little man, sitting cross-legged on the floor of his native hut. There was no talk then of his coming with me. He pleaded family business.

The joke of it all could really only be appreciated three years later. When the American Army liberated the Philippines in 1944, all these worms crawled forth from under their stones in their tens of thousands and, having found their uniforms again, stretched out their hands for back pay. Most of them claimed that they had been guerilla fighters and not only demanded their pay by right, but a medal if possible. They collected heaven knows how many hundred million dollars from that popular and public-spirited figure, the American Tax-payer.

In spite of the general demoralization, there were some Filipino Army officers who were real leaders of men. On Bataan, Philippine Army units, competently officered, had covered themselves with glory, and later, there was a young Colonel who led a guerilla band and became the terror of the Japanese on Panay. It was the tragedy of these men that their just claim to fame was endangered after the War by so many frauds.

For my money, the heroes of the landings in Iloilo had been two Filipino girls, in charge of the city's small telephone exchange. Of all the officials, civil and military, they alone stuck to their posts. When word came over the wire that Japanese landings had taken place at several points, they carried out their pre-arranged drill and warned all concerned until they could see the advancing enemy infantry from their windows. Then they put down their earphones and raced by back alleys to St. Augustine College, and only just made it.

As for me, I had been trapped again because I had acted too slowly and because I was buoyed up right to the end by false hopes that I might be able to organize an escape party. When I saw once again my friends carted away to internment, for a few days I felt like giving up the struggle and going with them. Verney saved me from that mood. Before he was taken away, he wished me luck, gave me three hundred pesos and told me to give his love to Australia. When I shook my head, he grew angry and told me to keep going. I did, and have always been grateful to him, although all my efforts to trace him and tell him so have been fruitless. I couldn't even find out whether he survived captivity.

The officers of "Hai Kwang" were interned, others got away to Negros and some were still free in the mountains of north-west Panay. But many of the British and Americans who lived at Jaro were tortured and killed.

During this time I stayed with the Augustinian Fathers, who hid me in their library whenever Japanese patrols came around. I was not a Roman Catholic, but they didn't mind that. On the contrary, it gave them a chance to try their great talents at proselytizing. Although I was impervious to their dogma, I was much impressed by their knowledge and persuasiveness, and if our many religious talks led nowhere, the Fathers gave me much valuable local information which came in handy afterwards.

By a stroke of luck I had heard that a Mr. Kinnes, an Englishman of Filipino nationality—there were such people—whom I had known in Kobe, now lived in a small barrio, or village, called Salog, on Guimaras Island across Iloilo Strait. Guimaras was unoccupied and likely to remain so. Since it was small, there was nothing of value there. The Japanese had sent only one patrol, which wisely stuck to the main village of BuenaVista, opposite Iloilo across the Strait. Mr. Kinnes and his daughter were quite happy to put me up, and I decided to go to them. But before I could leave Iloilo I had to have charts, a compass and other navigation aids. I also needed more cash.

Again I took advantage of my indeterminate national

51

status. The Japanese did not intern me, but they did not give me a pass to move around freely either. Meanwhile, before their system of civil control became fully established, I had to act quickly.

I secured a pass to visit the internees who had been put into the old Iloilo gaol and I saw them there daily for a week until my pass was withdrawn. During that time I was able to take them food and arrange lines of food supply for them.

From a sympathetic Spaniard I finally obtained some charts, a pair of dividers and a small four-inch boat's compass. And I still had my "Philippine Pilot" picked up on that hectic morning of the invasion.

I rode my luck with the Japanese. For two days I even acted as chauffeur to one of their senior officers and with him visited several Japanese Army installations. I was appalled to see the quantities and quality of supplies which had fallen into their hands. The burning of the city seemed to have been a senseless bit of arson when all that was of military value was left intact.

The Japanese were now beginning to be suspicious of me, and I was asked to report to the office of the headquarters of the Kempetai, the Military Police. It was obviously time to make myself scarce; so on 24th May, I said goodbye to the Augustinian Fathers and slipped through the back door of the city across Iloilo Strait to Guimaras Island.

I had wasted almost exactly four months on Panay.

III. SINGLE-HANDED VOYAGE

FINDING AND FITTING "MARING"

I FELT completely safe on Guimaras Island, although the Japanese garrison at Iloilo was only three miles across the Strait. The people were friendly and helpful; they had a grandstand view of the frightfulness at Iloilo, and had formed a genuine hatred and fear of the Japanese. Patrols could approach only by sea, and the villages—"barrios" as they were called—had all set up watching posts to give the alarm; and since the Japanese usually advertised their coming by flying flags from their boats, there was nothing to it. This watching system was adopted throughout the southern Philippines and enabled many people who would have attracted the unfavourable attention of the invaders to spend the next three years in comparative safety.

My plan for an escape had been taking on definite shape all through the hopes and disappointments of my last weeks in Iloilo, and in Guimaras I could at last go ahead. I had brought with me the money I had saved from my Iloilo job and this, together with Verney's three hundred pesos, would be enough to buy a modest boat and provision her. At last the initiative was with me.

I decided to buy my boat here in the Visayas—as the central islands of the Philippine Archipelago are called. Their "batils", round-bilged, double-ended boats with a fore-and-aft rig, would be excellent for single-handed sailing if I should have to make the journey on my own.

For months, in fact ever since I had first thought of an escape back in Manila, I had been considering the best route to take. I had talked to a great many people with local knowledge and had spent days and weeks weighing one thing against another until I now had my route worked out. I wrote the plan down in my diary in exact detail.

I intended to go south from Guimaras past the west coast of Negros, then due east over the Mindanao Sea and through Surigao Strait into the open Pacific, then south along the Mindanao east coast as far as the Sangir Islands. From there, south-eastwards across the top of the Molucca Passage past the east coast of Halmahera, then once again south-east, leaving Kofiaoe and Misool to starboard, striking south between Dutch New Guinea and Ceram, passing between the Kei and Tanimbar groups to Arnhem Land on the northern coast of Australia, then west to Port Darwin.

It was a roundabout route and a long one, but the alternative and more direct way through either the Macassar or the Molucca Passage would have been folly. These were established shipping routes, and were narrow and well-known waters which could be patrolled easily from bases such as Balikpapan, Samarinda, Macassar, Ternate and Ambon, now almost certainly in Japanese hands. Even if I succeeded in getting through either passage, I could be trapped in the narrow straits between the many islands stretching east from Java; and if, by incredible luck, I should manage to pass through that chain, there was still a long stretch of open water between those outer islands of the Netherlands East Indies and the Australian mainland. No, that route was impossible, and I was satisfied that my plan gave me at least a reasonable chance of getting through, although I remained sufficiently flexible in outlook to realize that weather and other unforeseen circumstances might dictate some deviations.

The next step was to find the sort of boat that would do the job and for which I could pay. Apart from the price, seaworthiness was the main consideration. Mere size in a boat has almost nothing to do with seaworthiness, and this was the point I could never get across to those of my friends

E

and acquaintances who at one time or another were thinking of coming with me. Seaworthy meant just that; the boat had to be able to keep the open sea. A boat twenty feet long —but not much shorter—could be seaworthy, and one which measured eighty feet could be a coffin which would drown you in the first blow.

Two questions had to be answered with yes before a hull could be considered seaworthy. First, was the underwater body sufficiently buoyant, and had the entrance at the stem, and exit at the stern, clean lines which made for smooth progress through the water? Second, was there enough freeboard, that is, height above water-line, to keep the boat dry under normal sailing conditions? Looking side-on, a hull had to have sheer to be seaworthy, a sweeping line coming downwards from the bow in a gentle curve to the waist of the ship, just behind the centre line, rising again gently towards the stern.

There were other considerations of seaworthiness, such as the proportion of width to length, the construction of the rudder and the way it was fastened to the boat. Another very important factor was the sail plan. A good sea-boat had to be fast enough to be easily and quickly manœuvred, but should not be over-canvased, or it would strain the hull when a bad sea was running. Too much sail would also make sail-handling difficult for one person. The boat had to be in reasonably good repair, the hull tight, with anchors and pump of reliable construction. It sounded an awful lot to ask, and beggars couldn't be choosers.

I was confident of my seamanship. I had been playing with small boats since I was twelve, and in Japan I had had excellent teachers. Racing I never liked much. When you raced, you either won a silver pot—not sterling either— or you broke your mast and strained the living hull of your beautiful ship. Blue-water cruising was for me. During the years in Japan I had gradually gained experience in sail-handling and manœuvring, provisioning and maintenance.

We had sailed in almost all weathers, over tricky patches, in confined waters and on the open sea. I had been through a good school.

In my search for a suitable boat I was lucky all the way. Mr. Kinnes introduced me to Patron, a Filipino Jack-of-all-trades who spoke good English and offered to help me find a boat, just for the fun of the thing. First I had a prahu—an outrigger canoe—in fair condition offered to me for sixty pesos. It was cheap enough, but I had to hold out for a round-bilged boat; a prahu would have been impossible during the coming season of the south-west monsoon. By luck I heard of a place called Nueva Valencia farther down the west coast of Guimaras, where there were reported to be a number of "batils" laid up. These stout double-ended vessels, rigged either as cutters or as sloops, were used for inter-island trading on a small scale.

With Patron and his brother I sailed in a prahu to Nueva Valencia, a distance of twenty miles. The sailing was a thrill. These sharp prahus with their bulky bamboo outriggers are very fast, but they require careful handling. A crew of three is the minimum, as one or two have to climb out on the windward outrigger to balance the boat with anything more than a gentle breeze blowing. We arrived around noon during heavy rain, to find that the news had been unreliable. There was only one old and decrepit tub for which the owner asked three hundred pesos.

But the trip was not wasted. Nueva Valencia appeared to be an ideal port to fit out in. It was a well-situated village, at the head of a shallow bay, and accessible only from the sea. The people were friendly and appeared anxious to help; the War was a long way off for them, and a mad stranger, looking for a boat to sail alone in, was a welcome distraction. There was plenty of fresh fruit around, and we gorged ourselves on mangoes and bananas.

We stayed overnight, and the next morning I saw a small sloop of about four tons, the "Rosita". She looked

57

just right, but her owner asked two hundred and fifty pesos, which was more than I could pay.

I blessed the Spanish, English or American carpenters of some generations ago, who must have taught the local ship-wrights how to build round-bilged boats with a European type fore-and-aft rig. Providence had certainly been kind to me. Nowhere else in the Philippines could I have hoped to find this type of boat, which could easily be sailed single-handed. All sea-going boats of native design required much man-power and a special skill in handling sails, which, to our ideas, were too large for the boats they drove and which were neither fore-and-aft nor square sails, but a combination of both.

Where there was one "Rosita" there would be others, and I decided to return to Salog to see whether I could raise some more money.

We travelled north again in our prahu through clear shallow water over coral gardens, which left the most vividly illustrated colour plates in natural-history books a long way behind, and we saw a sea snake, an ugly brute. We neared Salog at a roaring pace in a rising wind and barely escaped a black squall, short but fierce. We must have travelled over ten knots for a few minutes, a novel and exhilarating sensation.

On the following day I took the bit between my teeth and travelled across the Strait back to Panay, entering the little Iloilo suburb of La Paz via Loboc, a back door outside the Japanese arc of regular patrols. From Mr. Burgos, the loyal Spaniard who had previously obtained the compass for me, I raised another hundred pesos. I did not even have to sell my watch, as I had feared. He also gave me another chart which proved to be very helpful. This gentleman, for whom I had been able to do a service before the occupation of Iloilo, was a friend in need and made up for the hostile attitude of so many of his countrymen.

While I was in Iloilo I heard that the new civil Japanese

authorities were issuing permits to traders, and I had a brain wave. A Japanese trading permit might come in very handy. But was it worth the risk of walking into the dragon's jaws? I decided it was, and by a lucky chance I got into the building where the permits were issued without being challenged. I then did some fast talking which got me a piece of paper licensing me to buy and sell things; but coming out, a sentry scowled at me suspiciously and my heart gave a horrid bump. When I had got past, I felt that my luck couldn't hold much longer and if I should run into another sentry the game would be up.

That night I visited the home of an Englishwoman who was still free, although her husband had been interned. The news she told me about the War was bad. It appeared that all regular forces on Panay had surrendered, and she showed me a newspaper photograph showing General Christie in captivity.

On 29th May I left Panay for the last time and returned to Guimaras by prahu, crossing the Strait in ten minutes. Faithful Patron was waiting for me at our hiding-place among the mangroves.

I could not stay at the home of Mr. Kinnes any longer, the place was too close to Buena Vista, where the Japanese had already been once. I therefore decided to go to Nueva Valencia the next day, and Patron offered to come along with me. I could now afford to buy "Rosita".

Before leaving I bought provisions: rice, salt, sugar, some dried ginger, which would have to do for tea, and half a sack of mongo, a small pea not unlike lentils. The mongo took a lot of water to cook, but tasted delicious, especially with a pinch of salt. Two large bottles of kerosene and a brand new hurricane lantern, bought from Kinnes, were precious stores; so were the five boxes of matches which I kept in a tin with a tight lid. But I could get no tools, except for one hammer, some tacks and about a dozen nails, and I could get neither rope nor twine, only a ball of wrapping cord.

59

The moon was full and round that night and the weather ideal, but our start was inauspicious. After saying goodbye we sailed away, but quickly had to return for my hurricane lantern, which I had left on the beach. I had hired a larger prahu to take my belongings and provisions and we sailed quietly through the moonlit night, not far from the beach, with a gentle off-shore wind pushing us along. By midnight, when we were nearly at Nueva Valencia, heavy rain set in and drenched us completely. There was no tarpaulin or cover of any kind, and I feared for my rice. We anchored close to the shore feeling very miserable.

Next morning we reached Nueva Valencia to find that "Rosita" had gone, and another boat, which I had heard was also for sale, had left the previous day. The little port was empty again. But I was told that boats were constantly coming and going and I would be sure to find something, so there was nothing to do but wait.

The waiting was made easier by the spontaneous hospitality of the village folk. Our host was the Mayor, a kindly old man whom Patron knew. He and his wife shamed us by refusing to accept payment, even in kind, for food and lodging and seemed pleased and satisfied to stuff me with rice and with all the good things they had. Wherever I went in the Philippines, it was always the poor people who were the most helpful and hospitable. Whenever I tried to find out what was behind their indignant refusal to accept payment, I got the same reply: "It is nothing, please do not talk of it. One day I may travel and come to your country for hospitality." I met this attitude many times in the islands, among Christians and Moslems alike, and the poorer they were, the more they wished to share what they had.

The little township was typical of many in these outlying islands. Amid much natural wealth, there was dirt, poverty and ignorance. They had a Mayor, some Councillors and a Clerk, who banged a typewriter of sorts in the ramshackle Municipio, but the educational varnish was very thin, and hygiene and sanitation were extremely primitive. There were not even pit toilets, and the tide took care of the sewage. In earlier days the American administration had sent mobile Red Cross parties to the island to vaccinate and inoculate the population, and there was no longer any malaria.

We swam on a lovely white beach and we ate mangoes and eggs, rice and fish, all in plenty and fresh. We sailed in small canoes above coral formations of the most improbable shapes, and star fish and sea anemones so strange that I wondered whether they were animals or plants. It rained a lot, with that terrifying intensity only encountered in the tropics. Afterwards the sunsets were red and imposing, and I used to sit on a bleached log on the palm-fringed shore writing by the last rays of the sun as it set behind the mountains of Panay.

Words can never catch the beauty of sunsets like these. During the last ten minutes before the sun goes down the sky shows all the colours of the rainbow, down to the deepest purple, and in the strange light of the last few minutes before dusk the slender trunks of palm-trees, the drab colouring of the nipah houses on the shore, and even the usual rubble of coconut fronds and driftwood on the foreshore, all stand out in strong colours. The grass is greener than ever, the beach whiter and the yellow bamboo fences around the houses look as if they are lacquered and, as the wind dies, blue smoke curls up straight into the air from a dozen fires where the Filipinos are cooking their evening rice.

Patron was wonderful. He had scouts out far and wide, spreading the word that we wanted to buy a boat. But boat owners were becoming wise to smuggling possibilities, and their prices went up, or they refused to sell.

Traders passed with garbled news from the world outside. There were vague rumours of a big sea battle in the Coral Sea, and I secretly wondered whether Australia would be attacked. Of the war on the other side of the world, in Libya, the Near East, India, Burma and on the Russian front, I never heard a word for months.

I ought to have enjoyed the rest after the hectic last weeks at Iloilo, but my patience was getting ragged again. Of the hundred and forty days which had passed since I had left Manila, only ten had been spent in actually making good southing.

During the day I was never alone, but at night, tossing about on my mattress under the hot and stuffy mosquito net, doubts began to crowd in again. Suppose no boat was to be found? Risking it in a prahu would be certain suicide, and I was never one for that. Travelling in short stages was expensive, and even if I had enough money I could get no farther once I had reached the southernmost Philippines. But what alternative was there? I thought of returning to the unoccupied part of Panay and working and trading there until I had enough money to come back and buy the best boat I could find instead of buying now with my choice severely limited by my pocket.

On the fifth day of our stay at Nueva Valencia, Patron brought back what he called with fine understatement, "a little bit good news". He had arranged tentatively to buy the sloop "Maring" for two hundred and fifty pesos, subject to our inspection. The boat was coming back from Negros and was expected the next day. I had had too many disappointments to feel greatly excited.

"Maring" looked as if she could do it. She was a little double-ended sloop with a stumpy bow sprit. Her hull was strong and pear-shaped with the blunt part forward and the ends rather too fine for my liking. She had high free-board and a good sheer. Her exact measurements were 24 feet over all, 22 feet on the water-line, beam 7 feet 6 inches. Her draft was 2 feet 3 inches and, with ballast, could probably be brought to 2 feet 9 inches. The hull was well found and fully decked-in, with a cargo hatch measuring 3 feet by 5 feet to admit the thirty to forty bags of sugar, rice or corn with which her owners usually traded. Her keel was straight and her bilges round. She looked seaworthy enough, although she was not much longer than a good-sized rowing-boat.

Her gear above deck was a mess. In normal times I would have condemned the lot on sight. But there was nothing wrong with the sail plan. She was sloop rigged, with a high peaked gaff, the mains'l fairly large, but full of holes and patches. Her jib was rigged with a club and was in an equally poorly state. The standing rigging consisted of two wire shrouds with dead-eyes and lanyards, and one wire forestay. The wires were almost rusted through and the rope work was frayed. The single block of the jib halliard was so small and flimsy that if it had been on "Spray" I would not have trusted a signal halliard to it. Her most serious defect was a broken rudder gudgeon. But these were not basic faults, and could be repaired.

My relief at having a boat of my own at last was great, but it was tempered by the realization of how much work there was to be done to her.

On the following day I paid for "Maring" and took delivery of her. It happened to be the anniversary of my mother's birthday, and I took this as a good omen. What I was, I owed to her. In those far-away days in Hamburg she had had a boat herself, a lady-like little affair for paddling on the River Alster on a Sunday afternoon. My mother had always encouraged my sailing and playing with boats.

Patron and I had our first sail in "Maring", and found that she handled fairly well but seemed rather tender. As a yachtsman I had always sailed with a couple of tons of lead under the keel and that tended to deaden the "feel" for the tiller. It wasn't necessary to respond quite so quickly and meticulously to a strong wind. A keel yacht would just heel over and the lead in her keel would bring her back. "Maring" would have to be ballasted before she would sit firmly

63

in the water. I had also noticed that the local sailors were very quick about reefing and also pressed less, sailing with sheets more free than a yachtsman would. It was almost a year since the last time I had had "Spray's" tiller in my hand, and there was much to be learned again.

Fitting out was quite a job. For the next five days Patron and I worked at top speed, and I drove myself as much as I could. I did not want a Japanese patrol to come and spoil things at this late stage. At sea I would feel more secure.

We took the boat ashore at high tide to clean her and examine the underwater body, and word was sent to a blacksmith who came the next day and fixed the rudder gudgeon and an anchor stock. He also made me a traveller for the block of the main sheet, to move more easily across the top of the rudder.

Both sails were in a terrible condition, and I bought a small piece of sailcloth for which I had to pay dearly. Worst of all, I had neither sewing thread nor sail needles. The family of my host helped to mend the sails, or rather to patch them up. At sea I would have to make do with nails and wrapping cord. No Chinese junk in Hong Kong harbour had anything on me for patches.

Where to stow the water, and in what containers, proved one of the biggest headaches. I bought a sixty-gallon steel drum which had previously contained oil. This was to hold my main supply and, in addition, I bought two small stone jars, each holding approximately seven gallons. Fitting the drum correctly in the boat was vitally important. It had to be dead centre and in the right position fore and aft so that it would not disturb the boat's trim. It had also to be reasonably easy of access. Most important, it had to be so firmly secured that it would stay where it was. Some two hundred and fifty pounds coming loose in a seaway would be no joke. Fixing the drum was particularly difficult because we had only $1\frac{1}{2}$-inch nails and no sawn timber, but improvised chocks and struts were made and the drum stayed in place.

The pump was a quaint affair, simplicity and efficiency itself. It consisted of a hollow length of bamboo, with two leather flaps over either end, travelling in an iron pipe through the deck. Just to be on the safe side I had a spare pump made, and also bought a number of lengths of bamboo as general spares.

From my own experience and from books, I had come to realize that the success of a small-boat voyage depended to a great degree on the thoroughness of the preparations, and I tried not to overlook anything.

Patron worked hard and talked continuously. He had an extraordinarily alert mind, and we had many interesting discussions. He had been a dock-hand, a butcher, a farmer and what have you, he was about twenty-eight, but already had six children. They didn't waste much time hereabouts. He would have come along had it not been for his family, and this I understood. We never quarrelled, and I was angry with him only once. That was when he insisted on telling my fortune by reading my hand. He said he saw in the lines that my trip would be successful and I didn't mind that. But then he told me, in tones of the utmost finality, that I was not going to marry the girl I was engaged to. This struck me as absurd, but I didn't believe in palmistry, anyway.

"Maring" had to be ballasted. We put several hundred-weight of rocks aft and towards the centre, which the locals said would make her travel better. But I was sceptical, I thought that the ballast should be more evenly distributed and shifted some forward under the forepeak.

Stowing generally was a difficult job, because the boat lacked any interior shelves or lockers; there was just the shell of the boat and the gaping hole, the cargo hatch.

When the boat was ballasted we loaded my provisions and personal belongings on board. This was the full list:

Provisions

1 bag of rice, half polished, approximately 180 lb.
1 bag brown sugar, approximately 120 lb.
1 bag salt, approximately 80 lb.
½ bag mongo (lentils)
150 coconuts in the husk
15 tins, ½ lb. each, canned pilchards
1 tin jam
5 small tins of savoury meat paste
½ jar China tea
1 lb. dried ginger
Containers for 75 gallons water
50 mangoes, fresh
20 pineapples, fresh

Cooking and Eating Utensils

5 earthenware pots
Some sticks for ladles
Coconut shells for plates
2 empty 5-gallon tins, with a wire grill, draught hole and
    sand in bottom, as stoves
1 winnowing basket, for rice

Fuel, Lights and Matches

2 large bottles of kerosene
Provision for 100 bundles firewood
5 boxes matches in a tin

Tools and Spare Gear

1 bolo (long knife)
1 small hunting knife
1 hammer
Some 1½-inch nails
Brass tacks
About 20 square feet of cotton cloth for sail repairs

5 coils of about 20 feet each, $\frac{1}{2}$-inch hemp rope for spares
Several lengths bamboo for spares
Spare pump

Navigation Instruments

1 boat compass, 4 inches diameter, gimballed
1 pair of dividers
Charts—One of Malay Archipelago, taken from a Dutch
      Atlas
      Two maps from a Philippine Geography Book
      One large-scale map of Panay and Negros
      One map of Indian Ocean from "National
      Geographic Magazine"
1 "Philippine Pilot", Volume I
1 ruler
Pencils
Paper

Personal Belongings

1 kit-bag
1 haversack
1 leather brief-case
1 cotton blanket
6 grass mats
Mosquito net

I had been very lucky with my food supply and believed
that there was ample variety for all my needs. Fortunately
I had a fair idea of quantities per man consumed on small-
boat voyages, both from reading about them and from
experience.

The water supply would be sufficient. Even if I could not
replenish it anywhere, which was unlikely, I had enough for
almost a hundred days at the rate of more than half a gallon
a day. One gallon per day per man, I remembered, was the
Admiralty allowance, but that included water for washing.

Many small-boat sailors had written that half a gallon was just sufficient. Moreover, there was a fair amount of water in the coconuts—my iron reserve. At an average daily run of forty miles, a conservative estimate, I had enough water, even at the rate of one gallon a day, to cover the two thousand odd miles to Australia. But I was almost certain to be able to replenish *en route*.

Of sugar and salt I had, of course, too much, but I was told that both commodities could be used in the southern islands for barter against fresh fruit and fish, or whatever else might be available.

I should have liked to take some dried fish, but could not afford it after paying for firewood and giving a small token salary to Patron. I would be completely broke until I reached Australia.

My diary for 11th June reads:

> "Aboard sailing sloop 'Maring'. Patron and I left Nueva Valencia and anchored in a snug cove in Igang Bay to obtain firewood, stow everything and overhaul running rigging. I expect this to take another two days at the end of which will drop Patron ashore. The hoped for seems so far to have been accomplished. Am in excellent health, full of determination and good spirits. At Nueva Valencia I acted the trader and believe I aroused no suspicions, although people wondered why I took on so much water."

In Igang Bay we bought one hundred bundles of excellent firewood and stowed it under the forepeak. Matches were scarce and I learned to make a fire tolerably well in my only "stove", a converted rusty five-gallon tin. At sea, I observed that I didn't need my second "stove", and it became a useful storage tin for odd bits and pieces.

I didn't sleep too well that first night aboard. A hundred and one things went through my mind, and I continually sought for ways and means to improve the boat and

68

heighten the chances of success. I also had to get used to the rather hard hatch, as I had no mattress.

On 13th June we finished overhauling our running rigging and trimming the boat and shifted to Santa Ana, for the last bath and a rub down with soap and fresh water. I would probably miss washing most. I decided to try and shave at least once a week, but thought this a good opportunity to try and grow a moustache, something I had always wanted to do. As it turned out, it was a moth-eaten failure.

At Santa Ana we scoured and scoured the water drum to remove the last traces of oil. Then we filled it and our two stone jars with fresh water from the clearest well I had yet seen in the islands. I cut two wooden stoppers for the stone jars, and the steel lid was put firmly on the drum. This was necessary not only to prevent contamination, but to slow down evaporation and prevent slopping over. The stone jars were to supply my daily requirements and we lashed these on deck, aft, within good reach of the steering bench. Patron fashioned a neat little dipper out of a piece of bamboo.

At seven in the evening we anchored in Santa Ana Bay. All was ready and the last detail I could think of had been attended to when a very old man, taking us for traders, came alongside in an outrigger canoe. He asked for some salt and we gave him a coconut shell full.

The next morning I dropped Patron so that he could go back to Salog over an inland track. I thanked him as well as I could and gave him his miserable salary. He had been a wonderful helper, and I only wished I could repay him properly. All I could give him were fifteen pesos and my American razor. I had one five-peso bill left.

THE START OF THE VOYAGE

I was alone now. My diary became the official ship's log, and on 14th June I wrote:

"Prayed in the morning, and sailed out with the ebbing tide at 9.30 a.m., after saying goodbye to faithful Patron.

"As I raised the anchor and drifted out in a faint breeze, the old man to whom we had given some salt last night came tearing after me in his canoe and brought two fresh eggs in payment. When he saw that I was sailing alone, he broke into tears and, pointing to each of the two eggs in turn, sobbed 'Americano' and 'Filipino', then 'amigo' —friends. I believe he understood what it was all about.

"Am alone now and in His hands, but cannot be better cared for!"

The first night in the Panay Gulf was boisterous and I hove to with tight mainsheet and the jib backed. "Maring" lay quite comfortably that way and I slept. When I woke some four hours later the boat was still in the same relative position, drifting slowly downwind. The wind had been strong, but her decks were quite dry. My confidence in her grew. "Maring" had passed an important test of seaworthiness; she could be hove to and would stay that way. Not all small boats would do that.

On the second morning, the sea was fairly calm, but the sky was overcast. There was much to do and I had to settle in and establish my sea-going routine properly.

The first thing I decided to do every morning was to use the pump to see whether there was much water in the bilge. I was in for a shock when I discovered that the pump had no suction, although I could hear the water swishing about in the bilge. It did not take long to find out what had happened. I had shifted ballast too far forward so that she was out of trim and the water could not all flow to her stern. She was too far down by the bow, and the locals had been right about the necessity of sailing her on her stern. Why did I have to know better?

For five hours I sweated, shifting ballast. First I had to unload practically all the stores and leave them on deck, as

I had piled them on top of the ballast. Crawling in the confined space below deck and trying to shift large rocks was difficult, and I had never been a muscle-man. Moreover, since the boat was not lined with planks on the inside, I had to work very cautiously so as not to damage the planking. The job was eventually done but it cost me a day's run, and as well, I lost my working knife overboard.

Having finished below, I now took the first precaution necessary when sailing single-handed and tied a rope securely around my waist, belaying the other end of it with half turns and hitches to the foot of the mast. This left me plenty of freedom to move about and gave me a feeling of security. With no one to turn the ship around and pick you up again, falling overboard is one of the major hazards of single-handed sailing.

A small shark stayed with the boat all that day, playing around the rudder and feasting on the small fish always to be found there. The run was only twenty-one miles. No sail was in sight.

At the outset navigation was quite simple. I had only to follow the coastline of Negros south, and it was easy to recognize the mountains and bays marked on the map. I kept to sea at a distance of fifteen miles from shore, true to the motto of that great yachtsman, Claud Worth, who first said that "The Sea is Kind to Little Ships".

At night I hove her to again to get some sleep and woke at four in the morning. She sailed beautifully to a sweet-smelling and steady night breeze from the land, and I began to feel happy and did not mind at all being alone. There was so much to do and to think about.

In the afternoon a heavy rain squall came up, but I did not dare to press the boat in the strong wind that accompanied it. Right from the start I had to nurse the old sails and the running rigging. I could not cook myself any supper and the scene became miserable again. It rained all evening.

Next day, I tackled the business of making a fire. I had

managed all right ashore when there was nothing else to think about, but on a moving boat, in rain and wind, it was quite different. And the tiller couldn't be left for long either.

I spent hours at it. Again and again I built small mounds of kindling, shavings and dry coconut husks, which burnt well and glowed like cinders, but after a brief flicker the flames always died again. I could not afford to waste matches, and I blew and blew until I became purple in the face and dizzy with the fumes. Even a few drops of my precious kerosene did not help at first. I had never been the Boy Scout type, and was used to doing my cooking afloat on a gimballed Primus stove. I felt a fool, but finally got on top of it—just in time to have my breakfast at noon. Then my gear became wet again and the rice did not look too good either, so I had to stow and restow again. This was my baptism in long-distance voyaging, and I still had a lot to learn.

But one thing I knew from the beginning, health was of the first importance. I had read too many stories of small-boat trips which had had to be abandoned because the crew became sick not to take this seriously. Living for weeks in a space not much larger than a billiard table brings its own health problems—for a start, most yachtsmen become constipated the moment they step on board. That alone is a handicap to complete fitness, and I had to be in first-class physical condition to be able to cope with navigation and manoeuvring the boat for at least eighteen hours out of the twenty-four. I had been brought up on the principle that man eats to live and not the other way round, but here, on board, food and drink became my foremost concern, equal in importance to navigating the boat.

I intended to keep strictly to fixed meal-times. At eight in the morning I had coconut meat with brown sugar. The fire was lit at ten for a brew of ginger "tea" which took getting used to, but supplied warmth and vitamins. Patron had shown me how to make it by beating a thumb-sized piece of ginger with the handle of the bolo until it became mushy and then boiling it with brown sugar "to taste", as they say. After making the "tea" the mongo were put on; they needed over an hour's boiling and had to have water added constantly. I had my dinner of mongo at noon and cooked rice for supper at six. The stove and the firewood required for the day were kept handy near the steering bench, and I could keep an eye on the fire and pots as I steered. The only matches used were for fire-making in the morning, and after some days, I was expert enough to use only one match a day. This became a point of honour.

My diet was as varied and well-balanced as I could make it. While the fresh fruit from Nueva Valencia lasted, I feasted. The few tins and the China tea which I had brought were for special treats or emergencies. Long and dangerous small-boat voyages had been made on much less food and, barring accidents, my food stock gave me no cause for anxiety.

All this first week I lost much time because I constantly had to rearrange my stores in the boat until I discovered the most satisfactory method of storing them; and when the sun came out and it was calm the boat looked like a Chinese laundry with clothes and gear laid out and hung up to dry.

Another thing which I learned gradually was the knack of letting "Maring" steer herself with a tiller rope without my having to touch the helm, and she sailed quite well for several minutes with the wind abeam or slightly forward, and was excellent with a quartering breeze. But getting the boat to steer herself for longer periods was vitally important, if it could be done. If she could be made to sail for several hours while I slept or cooked or worked at my navigation, it would make all the difference to the time I took to reach Australia.

No two boats are alike in this respect; there is no magic formula to teach you how to set sail and adjust the rudder so that a boat will steer herself. Some ships do it easily, some never at all. Others do it only if the wind is from a certain direction, and they come up to windward when it changes. It depends on a lot of things, the shape of the hull, the centre of effort of the sail plan and on other structural factors.

I experimented with different courses and sail settings and finally got the boat to look after herself tolerably well. This was achieved by passing a rope with a double hitch secured to the tiller and fastening it on both sides of the boat, athwart ship, thus fixing the tiller in a certain position. Like this "Maring" would sail by herself for about fifteen minutes, but never much more.

The famous Captain Joshua Slocum—spiritual father of all single-handed yachtsmen—maintains in his book that his "Spray" used to sail for weeks unaided across the Pacific in the trade winds. I had tried to copy him in a smaller way in my own "Spray" in Japan before the War but never made it. Now, after my experiences in "Maring", I began to doubt whether he had been telling the truth, the whole truth and nothing but the truth.

The weather was fickle during those first few days, and this was perhaps as well, for I learned much about the behaviour of my boat in all winds. June was reputed to be the season of south-west monsoons, but for four days the winds blew from every other quarter. I was probably still a little too far north to be in the monsoonal belt.

When the heavy squalls blew out from the coast towards evening I had to get the sails right off her. I could not risk any fancy sailing with that canvas. The club jib was not much of a success. I took the club off and belayed the sheets to a pin in the bulwark, close to the shrouds.

The weather continued to be abominable. There were ugly nights and mornings, the kind when I wished I had taken to breeding white mice instead of taking up sailing. The grass mats could not keep the rain out and the inside of the boat became impossible. There was no ventilation, and smells of many origins wafted up the hatch. The clothing I used to dry when the sun shone around noon was wet through again a few hours later. Wood lice or some such vermin had a lot of fun below decks. I gave up sleeping down there and preferred the rain and wind up top.

But it wasn't all black. My confidence in the behaviour of "Maring" grew each day. In the squalls she rolled her decks in at times, but otherwise rode them out in style. Once I saw a Japanese plane going to Mindanao. This scared me a little because the noise was quite unusual. Otherwise the sea and coast were deserted, there was not even a sail to be seen. It seemed quite unlikely that a Japanese party patrolling along the shore would be met as far out as I usually sailed, but for safety a fire was taboo after dark, as I never knew whom the glow might attract. Only the embers stayed alive long enough to keep my pipe going until nine o'clock. Later-on I was to learn the trick of keeping a fire alive overnight in a dry coconut husk which could be made to glow like charcoal for many hours.

On the 18th June, the northern coast of Mindanao was in good view. It had taken me five days to cover only ninety-five miles and at this rate, it would take me eighty days to reach Australia. This was not good enough. But the next day I hoped to round the southernmost point of Negros, then turn north-eastward and make good time across the Mindanao Sea for Surigao Strait.

But things didn't work out that way. For a full week, while I tried to battle my way eastward, I stayed more or less in the same spot. The mountains of Negros in the north and of Mindanao in the south looked at me day after day until I hated the sight of them. I simply could not get through that fifty miles of sea between them.

The log tells the story:

"*19th June.* Last night when cold, wet and miserable, thought of Captain Bligh, how much better I still had it. He had many men, an open boat, no fire, little water and provisions.

75

"*20th June*. Was in a blue funk yesterday afternoon, thought of turning back. Pump rod broke. Wind adverse. Discovered boat very bad in windward work with any sea running. Cannot keep her hold dry. Rudder gudgeon loose again.

"This noon still far S.W. of Negros S. point. Will I ever get round it? Calm and hot now. Boat tumbling in confused swell like a drunk.

"Had fine W. wind all afternoon, but wasted, as I used it to get back distance lost yesterday and last night.

"Discover being alone not so easy for my temperament.

"Sleep is the big problem, I can cope with the navigation, sailhandling and cooking, but have so little time for sleep. Must not sleep during the day for fear of patrols, and at night the wind is usually so good and steady that I cannot bring myself to waste it and do not lower sails until I literally drop down. If hurry were not essential, how pleasant it could all be! Now I lose too much time when I lower sails at midnight, or 2 a.m., and never sleep more than four hours, for the wind usually freshens before sunrise on a fine day and holds until about 10 a.m.

"Have become accustomed to the routine of meals, and shall stick to two hot feeds a day, and one hot drink. Ashore one could do with one hot meal, but single-handed sailing consumes energy and makes sufficient food a condition *sine qua non*. Getting better at the fire. On several days now I have succeeded in using one match only per day. The firewood is excellent, but I am not good with the bolo, chopping it.

"*21st June*. One week and have not yet rounded Negros, but am in process of doing it now, close along coast to avoid a current apparently setting west further out to sea. Spoke to two natives in a canoe who wanted to buy corn or rice from me. Heavy rain all morning. Will I ever get out of this bad-weather corner?

"Dropped all 'yachty' customs, deck scrubbing,

meticulous serving of each rope-end and the official log suffers. Shall have more than enough to do to keep myself well fed and sail the boat. Wish I had six hands.

"Gradually discovering how to do four things at the same time, for instance, watch the fire, sail, read charts and write this log.

"Boat an awful roller. Cannot keep on hatch at night. Therefore invented what I shall call 'Klestadt's Patent Scupper Bunk'. The deck between hatch coaming and bulwark is just wide enough to squeeze in my 'bed', a sort of bamboo grille which gives at least an illusion of softness. Am thus firmly chocked down. Only disadvantage—wet in rain and when she rolls her sides under, which is often.

"Cleaned fingernails because Sunday, but did not shave.

"Wonderful sailing at last. Cleared Negros with a fresh breeze dead aft. Doing 4½ knots and sailed twenty miles since noon. Course now west by north to Surigao Strait.

"*22nd June*. Yesterday's joy short-lived. The wind petered out towards sunset and during night lost about ten miles drifting S.W. while I slept.

"Raining again, and calm. It is exasperating!

"All things becoming mouldy including myself. Since leaving eight days ago there has not been one day entirely without rain.

"Saw my first two steamers today. They passed fairly close by, but did not bother even to look. There was hardly any wind at the time and I was a fine target. Badly scared.

"Afternoon. Have lost all I gained yesterday and more by drifting to the S.W. Am back again near Negros S. point. Eight days out. Hardly 110 nautical miles made good on an 1800 miles course!

"Am thinking again of returning, but both ways seem

so impossible! I am truly in torment, and have a mind to let the first steady breeze decide for me.

"Evening. Quiet upon the waters. How can I turn back and steer north, when everything worthwhile is south?

"And yet the practical difficulties are appalling!

"After only eight days out, the sail has suffered terribly and is more holes than anything else. There is hardly one reef point sound, ditto the halliards and sheets! Yet I am short of spares and already adopting the most fantastic make-shifts! Her bottom is foul, which retards progress— the growth is incredibly quick here! One rudder gudgeon is loose! And all for 110 miles in eight days! How shall I carry on after leaving the Philippines when the only chart I shall have is a page torn from an atlas?

"Oh Lord, make me strong, that I can do Thy Will.

"Spent three hours today mending a tear a foot long in the mains'l. Having neither twine nor proper sail needles, I had to make the holes with a nail and thread them with wrapping cord like a shoelace. If I had not felt like crying I would have laughed. It looked so funny and unseaman-like.

"*23rd June.* This morning caught a tiny crab which had sought shelter on my rudder. I speared it with my bolo, fried the poor thing and had at least a faint reminder of the taste of fresh fish! Yes, with the bolo, a unique instrument and probably the Filipinos' only contribution to civilization. It is a sort of bush-knife, four inch handle, the blade about a foot long, $2\frac{1}{2}$ inches wide and tapering off to a point. With it you can conveniently split open coconuts, cut firewood, clean fingernails, sharpen pencils, cut off heads and do almost anything for which we re-quire half a dozen different weapons. It is moreover my only knife, since I lost my small sheath knife.

"Later. This had been another hot day of calms, fears and indecision. I have now drifted so far to the southwest that I am seriously considering cancelling Surigao and sailing along the northwest coast of Mindanao and Zamboanga instead. Right now am steering that direction to a light W. breeze. I shall let the first strong breeze decide. It seems the S.W. monsoon, on which I had counted to blow me along to Surigao, does not become settled for a week or two yet. I doubt all books now.

"Evening, after another day on which I could not hear the lap-lap of the wake, or see the flying fish rise. But my spirit is still unbroken and, strangely, I feel I am over the hump. These first days have not been easy. Fortunately, I am completely healthy. Attribute my health solely to the regular meals to which I cling, however tired I may be. The rice in particular is very nourishing, being only half-polished. It is called 'red' rice, a Panay variety, which does not taste as smooth as the big-grained Japanese 'kome'. Have become used to cooking it just right. Wash twice in salt water and then put it on an even heat. Even heat and the right amount of water is the whole secret. Keeping a constant fire has become quite a hobby and when it rains I rig up some mats which at least shelter the stove.

"Why will people eat refined sugar and polished grains which have had much of their food values extracted? The coconuts take a bit of munching down, but the younger ones are quite good. Mongo are a treat.

"*24th June*. Still between Negros and Mindanao but further southwest than before. Now it has started to blow a bit from that quarter, but I shall try to close with the Mindanao coast and then work close-shore. Shall open a tin of pilchards to celebrate when I am well on the way to Zamboanga and out of this messy place.

"Made bad discovery: some rice mouldy! Must dry all in calm weather. More work! There is a foul smell in the boat. Apparently the bark of some of the firewood has rotted in the bilge water. Bad stowing. It takes time, trial and error before the routine in any boat, however

79

small, has shaken down properly. Have to pump her dry twice a day, first and last thing in the morning and evening, she still draws too much through the planking. The trouble is that she has no floor boards, which means that the bulky firewood and coconuts have to be stored in the bilge.

"The water drum gives no trouble and does not budge, and the water tastes as good as the day we took it on. Just as well!

"Noon. Drifting in an oily swell. How well I can understand the exasperation of Alan Villiers who hung around this same Sulu Sea for many days in the 'Joseph Conrad'. He saw the same half-empty tin float in the same position near the ship for days and finally got so exasperated that he lowered a boat and pushed the damn thing under! This story has stuck in my mind and I always find it difficult to believe. Even now, in almost the same spot, there is always some difference in the rate of drift of different objects, and at this moment I find I am slowly, inch by inch, passing a piece of wood which has been close by for an hour.

"*25th June*. No change! After crawling all yesterday to within five miles of the Mindanao coast, last night I was thrown back again about twenty miles by a heavy squall from the mountains called a colla in the pilot. Had quite a time lashing sails and spars without damaging them, as I left it too late, hoping to claw some way to windward under reefed sail. It was no use. The squall broke too quick and strong for carrying any sail with this gear. It is a wonder nothing serious has carried away yet. I had, however, sufficient time to judge her sailing reefed. She is a thoroughly bad egg. Without jib, she will not pay off, and with it, she carries lee-helm. Have no storm-jib, and cannot reef the working jib.

"It was a boisterous night with the wind piping its proverbial tune in the shrouds and 'Maring' was pressed fairly well over. But when it calmed down after midnight there was nothing to steady her and she tumbled about ducking her decks in and drenching me with spray and blue water. I was already wet to the skin from the rain. Got up this morning with stiff joints and swollen eyes, but a hot meal and the sun fixed things quickly.

"It is always a wonder and a heart-warming surprise to see a little ship come through a night like that un-damaged, clean and chastised, with her lines taut with the wet. Last night it looked a bit grim for a time with spars rolling about, sails flapping and ropes blowing out to leeward. But after everything had been lashed down, 'Maring' looked after herself better than I could have done. A good little ship, how right was the man, who-ever he was, who said that a good ship will stand up to more than any man has the nerve to put her to.

"Now it is calm again and wet clothes are drying. The usual routine. Have now definitely decided to return if I am not well on my way either to Surigao or Zamboanga within one week. The gear just won't stand it. Shall then run back to Guimaras and try to make some money trading with 'Maring' until I can fit her out better.

"The sail should come down in this calm, but have an obsession to close with the coast."

SOUTH-WEST MONSOON

I took the line of least resistance and gave up my attempts to reach the open Pacific via Surigao Strait. Instead, I decided to sail along the west coast of Mindanao, past the Zamboanga Peninsula, and then pass eastwards through the Celebes Sea.

Late at night on 26th June I closed with the Mindanao coast near Dapitan and ran close inshore, anchoring for the first time since leaving Guimaras twelve days before. That night I slept to the music of cocks crowing and crickets

81

chirping and, in the morning, made sail again before sunrise to a light breeze which lasted all day. From the lay of the land I judged that we were in Sindangan Bay.

Still it rained, and the next night I slept again in sodden clothes. I did not mind the wet so much for myself, but I was much afraid for my rice and other provisions, as the deck leaked in several places.

"Maring" went poorly to windward and the next day's run in the light wind was hardly ten miles. At night I anchored again off the coast, but this time in front of a village and, before going to sleep, I was hailed from a canoe by a Filipino. He spoke good English and told me that the name of the village was Karakol. Then he came close and appeared to regard me with suspicion mixed with a certain respect for my sailing alone, but ended up with a friendly invitation to spend the night in his house. I was so fagged out and so charmed by the prospect of a dry sleep that I accepted and left the boat at anchor in a fairly well-protected little bay. It was the first time in twelve days that I had gone ashore, and I felt quite unsteady on my legs.

A small crowd had gathered on the beach to witness the arrival of a crazy white stranger who sailed alone—probably after murdering his shipmate. This suspicion was a cross I had to bear throughout the single-handed trip. I soon found out that violence was so much an accepted condition of people's lives in this southernmost part of the Philippines that since they never sailed alone themselves, the only reasonable explanation they could think of for my doing so was that I had done away with my companion.

As in other parts of the Philippines, the commercial element even in this small community was supplied by the Chinese owner of the little village store. He was among the crowd which welcomed me, and he invited me to his store and offered me a glass of real coffee, piping hot, which tasted wonderful after my ginger tea. Then my Filipino host led me through some coconut groves to his palm-thatched house. The earth smelt very sweet after the rain, we had a wonderful meal of bananas and fried fish, and the world was a good place to be alive in.

The next day I cleaned the underwater body of the boat with the help of a young Moro boy. While we scraped off the small barnacles and algæ which had grown since Nueva Valencia and were dragging at her speed, the bystanders gave good advice and solemn warnings. They told me that Moro pirates were operating near Zamboanga and that various unpleasant things would happen to me if I should be unlucky enough to fall in with them. As if worrying about interception and capture by the Japanese wasn't enough! But the boy helping me was not so gloomy. He told me that Sangboy Island was a friendly place to stop and said that he was going the next day by vinta and would be there when I arrived. While I was mending the sails as best I could, a Moro fisherman came along and presented me with four fresh fish fried in coconut oil, and I gave him some sugar in return. I began to feel hopeful again.

This encounter at Karakol was my first meeting with the famous Moro race, which is quite different from the Filipino. Moro men are taller, with lean figures and cat-like movements, and where the faces of Filipinos are soft and pleasant, the Moros have harder features and their eyes burn right through you.

Although I was still well within the territory of the Philippine Commonwealth, I was actually on the border line of a different country. I had heard quite a bit about the Moros, their seamanship and their quick tempers and religious fanaticism. They are mostly Moslems and have a standing feud with the Christian Filipino settlers in Mindanao. The Moros I encountered were the descendants of the braves who had attacked small steamers from their swift-sailing vintas only some sixty years before and whose piratical and murderous exploits were told throughout the eastern world. Only a generation or two earlier they had

83

sailed from the northernmost Philippines across the equator as far south as Timor, and from the Solomons in the east to Achin on Sumatra in the west, striking terror into the coastal villages and towns.

Now the boat was clean, it was time to leave Karakol, but before I sailed, I bartered sugar in exchange for bananas, and the Chinese storekeeper made me a present of twenty-two eggs.

It still rained a lot, but gradually the weather improved and my spirits with it. I was glad to be at sea again and enjoyed the sailing until I gave myself a good gash in the left hand with my bolo, which made sail setting quite difficult for a time. For a couple of days, two sharks played about the boat; they were the largest I had yet seen, each about five feet long, and one of them had whitish fins and two broad black stripes like a zebra. I threw coconut husks overboard to see whether they would bite, but they were not amused and, for my part, the temptation to swim from my boat, even when anchored, was easily resisted.

Sailing along the Zamboanga Peninsula was idyllic for a few days. The wind was light during the daytime, but there was always a strong and steady off-shore breeze coming down from the mountains at night. This made for excellent sailing because the water was quite smooth in the lee of the land. Several times I sailed through the night, and slept by day.

One evening when I had anchored close to shore to await the evening breeze, a Moro vinta came up next to me. I gave the crew some sugar and bananas "to make goodwill", as my brother used to say when he waved to fishermen from "Spray", and admired her beauty. She was about twenty feet only, canoe-shaped, with pointed ends and fine lines. Her lower hull appeared to be carved from a single tree of a whitish sort of wood, and two cross beams supported the bamboo outriggers, which curved upwards at the forward end like a sleigh. Her sharp bow and stern were decorated with a filigree pattern of scrolls and curves, not unlike the designs on damaskeen ware. Under her large square sail, every line of this graceful boat spoke of a living tradition of skill and craftsmanship.

I lived quite royally while the eggs and bananas lasted. My cooking improved and when I made scrambled eggs they were a rousing success—the last time I had tried them had been in "Spray's" galley. My stock of bananas looked like going bad, so I experimented. I cooked them with their skins in salt water, which was good. I baked them in the ashes of the dying fire as a late supper snack, which was even better. Then I sliced and boiled them with sugar and water as a kind of stewed fruit, but that was awful. I am sure I should have discovered other delicious methods of cooking them if I had had a frying-pan. If it had not been for fatigue, anxiety about running into Moro pirates and the ever-present fear of interception by the Japanese, I could almost have believed myself on a pleasure cruise.

I was nearing the tip of the Zamboanga peninsula when a large Japanese freighter passed well out to sea. All the same, I held my breath. That same night I heard the noise of a motor. When it went on for two hours I thought it must be a rice mill, the type found in most villages in the islands. But it wasn't a rice mill. Two days later, I heard the identical noise again and soon saw where it came from: a Japanese patrol boat! I was afraid to alter course when it approached for fear of attracting attention, and we passed on opposite courses about two cable lengths apart. "Maring" looked inconspicuous and commonplace in those waters, and I was all muffled up in my raincoat with the light behind me, but I could plainly see their faces and that hated flag, the Rising Sun, painted on the hull and flown from the stern. They didn't take any notice of me, but it was the worst fright of the trip so far.

It was about this time that I came to terms with myself and the trip I had embarked on. Ever since leaving Guimaras in

"Maring", the colours of the sea and the coast had held a strong fascination for me, and on this particular afternoon I remember clearly a passing shower just before sunset and the full rays of the sinking sun lighting up a golden beach and the green hills beyond. "Maring" was sailing sweetly, and I thought how beautiful the earth was and what a mean place we often made of it.

There had been times when I was lonely and appalled by the task ahead. But now, for the first time in my life, I felt completely at peace with myself and there came over me an exaltation such as I had never experienced before. I saw myself engaged in a clean and clear-cut fight. I was my own master, and salvation depended only on me. If my seamanship and navigation, my strength and wit were good enough, I could get through. This voyage was a test of strength, and there was great satisfaction in tackling it. Interception by the Japanese—that was a chance I had to take. I could try to avoid those places where they were most likely to be found in numbers, but that was all.

The exaltation did not remain long at its first peak of intensity, but I never quite lost it afterwards. I felt that this moment was the high-water mark of my life. Whatever had gone before and whatever was to follow would never quite equal the joy of living I experienced that afternoon. There was nothing mean or petty in that fight on the water. "Maring" and I were alone under the heavens, and nothing could harm me as long as I obeyed the laws of God.

From that moment onward I felt a strength and confidence which never quite left me.

Now the south-west wind freshened and I had to tack a lot, "Maring's" weak point. One day I sailed more than twenty miles but made good only eight on my course because I had to take long legs up wind. I saw more Japanese steamers passing, two modern freighters and a tanker, but I now realized that these large vessels were unlikely to bother about a small native boat. It was the patrols I had to look out for.

On 3rd July I came to anchor in a tiny corner of Siocun Bay. During the short time before dusk I had worked up to the head of a snug little inlet, coming to anchor over the clearest water I had yet seen around here. Although it was rapidly getting dark, the anchor and warp, some twelve feet down, were as clearly visible as on dry land, and as I bent over the bulwark, "Maring" seemed to float in space. The shore was closely wooded down to the water, and monkey chatter, the screech of tropical birds invisible in the thick foliage and a fiery sunset have left the scene clear in my memory.

After dark, some natives hailed the boat from shore, first in Tagalog, the Philippine's most widely used native language, then in English and finally in Spanish. I did not answer; the less I came into contact with anybody, the better. I was too near Zamboanga town, which I knew was garrisoned, to take unnecessary risks.

This anchorage was truly a bit of luck. At night the water looked like a sheet of glass, reflecting the brightness of the stars. "Maring" did not move. I turned in for a full eight hours' sleep and sailed with the pre-dawn breeze the next morning.

Still my rice and my clothes got wet and had to be dried again. It wasn't quite as easy as it sounded. The rice had to be poured on an empty bag and then transferred in small quantities to a winnowing basket on which it had to be shifted frequently. The boat remained very wet and I moved ballast again. I brought her down by the stern still farther so that the maximum of water would flow aft where the pump could get it out. I counted two hundred and fifty strokes of smelly bilge water before she was clear. I christened my pump "Caleb Bilge-Water" after a poem I had once read.

Despite all my care, some tropical ulcers developed on my legs and mosquito bites became infected by flies and refused

G

to heal. They did not hurt—except when they touched a sharp object—but were a nuisance and took the edge off my fitness, besides cleaning and bandaging the ulcers every day took time, and there was not enough of that. Mercuri-chrome, I found, was the only remedy I had which did them any good. My "medicine chest", bought in a drug store in Manila shortly before I left, was a Boy Scout outfit, a little tin box that fitted to the belt and contained some bandages, sticking plaster and a small bottle of mercurichrome. I had also bought a bottle of hundred aspirins and a small flask of iodine.

As we sailed down the peninsula there were more Moro vintas about and, although I was always on the alert, re-membering all the warnings against Moro pirates in this area which had been impressed on me at Karakol, none of them made any attempt to molest me. It was just as well. "Mar-ing" and I wouldn't have stood a chance if one of them had given chase.

I was fascinated by the astonishing speed of the vintas and their strange sails. Their sail plan was a combination of square sail, fore-and-aft and lugger. I had never seen any-thing like it before. The square sails had much belly and were marled to two spars, which could be described as upper and lower yards, or boom and gaff, as they performed similar functions. The whole affair was hoisted slantwise to a stumpy mast and was worked with gaskets, lifts and braces. The nearest sail plan in the western world is a lateen rig, except that the lateen sail is triangular and the Moro sail square.

The proportion of sail to the size of the hull was fantastic by our standards. The whole effect could be described as a huge sail with a bit of wood under it to keep it afloat. And the performance of these vintas was extraordinary. In the slightest whisper of a wind, when clumsy "Maring" would stand motionless, the vintas would sail past at four or five knots. In a breeze and properly ballasted, these boats could make speeds of up to fifteen knots, and probably more. It wasn't sailing at all as we know it, but more like toboggan-ing over the surface of the water, or ice sailing. One man would steer and four or five would balance away up on the outriggers to keep the vinta level. Now at last I could under-stand and believe the tales of Moros invariably outsailing their pursuers.

Travellers who have described the Moros and their sailing skill have written rapturously about these men and their boats, but many of them have gone on to disparage all other forms of sailing having forgotten to mention the vintas' limitations.

For acrobatic fair-weather sailing and speed these Moros and their boats could beat anything afloat without an engine, they would certainly make the most over-canvased Sydney harbour dinghy look like the slow boat to China. But there was a difference between their method of sailing and ours. The boys down here were fair-weather sailors, and this is not meant as a criticism. With rare exceptions, they did not keep the sea but sailed close to shore, or from island to island, by the most direct route. Also, the weather in these equatorial parts was mostly light when they travelled and the squalls lacked the weight of those in our colder and harder latitudes. In really bad weather, in a typhoon or major storm, these boats could not live in the water at all.

With "Maring" wallowing about in an early morning calm, I would enviously watch the vintas glide past as if driven by silent engines; but for all-weather sailing I would choose a round-bilged boat any day, with a bit of weight on the keel if possible.

But we had our moments too, "Maring" and I. There were mornings when the wind would die down at nine o'clock and it would get steamy and hot. "Maring", with-out the steadying hand of the wind on her, would flounder about like a drunk and I would sit by the useless tiller doing odd jobs, fretting, and feeling hot and uncomfortable with a sweaty and none-too-clean shirt sticking to my back and the sun beating down. I would be squinting in the glare from the smooth water and know that a headache wasn't far off.

Then, suddenly, half a mile away, a blue ripple would show up, and a thin dark line appear on the horizon, and I would put away what I had been doing and sit at the tiller to wait for my friend, the wind. At once my face would be touched with coolness and gradually the tiller would come to life until the boat was bowling along with a bone in her teeth and her wake gurgling with pleasure.

But the wind wasn't too kind to us near the southern end of the peninsula. It started blowing again from the south-west, the quarter where I wanted to go. Sailing in a head wind always meant useless tacking, as "Maring" would not lay closer to the wind than six or seven points in anything of a swell and a breeze; so, rather than strain my dilapidated sail unnecessarily I would make for the coast and anchor. Doing it alone was fun, it was a game of seamanship versus unknown ground and currents.

Whatever size ship you anchor, the manœuvre is always the same in principle. You select a berth with careful thought for depth, shelter and how-to-get-out-again. Then headsails are lowered. You approach the chosen spot and drop the hook carefully, neither throwing the warp on top of it nor letting the anchor warp and tripping line foul each other. Then the mains'l comes down. You pay out warp or chain, as the case may be, to about three times the depth of water and make everything shipshape, stowing sail properly. Alone, anchoring can be tricky when the boat has speed on, especially in restricted waters where the type of bottom is not known. The colour of water is the best depth indicator, and in time I learned the knack. I usually lashed the tiller and let her work up slowly, conning from the bow. Once I had to lower the jib while running fast, and this required careful tiller adjustment and nippy work. When on the wind,

"Maring" could not be persuaded to pay off again without her headsail.

My ground tackle worried me at times. "Maring" had only one small fisherman-type anchor and some fifty feet of seven-eighth-inch hemp warp. Normally, that would have been sufficient, but coral, beautiful to look at, is needle-sharp and vicious to anchor over, especially at night, and I often wished I had at least four feet of chain close to the anchor. I had bent a tripping line to one anchor fluke and had been very fortunate so far. Twice I had to sail the anchor out, as I had no dinghy; this was a dangerous manœuvre which could have cost me an anchor, but luck was with "Maring" every time.

On 4th July I anchored in Sibuko Bay in a snug berth lying close to the shore and listened to the birds singing and the monkeys gossiping while I cooked my evening rice. In the evening of 5th July after a pleasant day's sailing I passed Batorampon Point, the westernmost extremity of Mindanao. For the next eighteen hours the wind held fair and I pushed the boat along. During the day I saw another modern Japanese steamer, which appeared to be of the Yamashita or "K" class cargo type, camouflaged with dazzle paint. They did not have too many of those beautiful ships to lose.

That night I passed the latitude of Zamboanga City, keeping well to the westward, and in the morning I was to the north-west of Basilan Island opposite Zamboanga, on a course to Pilas Island. There were strong currents and confused seas in this chain of islands dividing the Sulu and Celebes Seas.

About two o'clock in the afternoon a squall struck. It came from due south and boiled up the already confused water even more. I intended to round the west and south coasts of Basilan, but it became quite impossible in that wind. When the squall persisted and blew up into what passed down here for half a gale, tacking with a ship that would lie only seven points to the wind and pitched twice into the same hole became sheer self-deception. I had to run her off with sheets free and we made to the west, seeking shelter in the lee of tiny North Sangboy Island, one of the many islands of the Pilas Group. And here I ran straight into Moro land.

About fifteen vintas had had the same idea and were already at anchor. I did not know what I had struck; these people were something new and different. All Moros look fierce with their teeth blackened from chewing betel nut and the corners of their mouths constantly dribbling blood-red juice, but these were a particularly savage-looking lot. Unlike other Moros I had seen on Mindanao, these were almost naked, and they were utterly filthy. The men had on G-strings and the women sarongs. Their tiny boats were apparently their homes, for they carried their whole establishment in them.

Because of the narrowness of the anchorage I had to lie near them and they tried to make contact. I wasn't quite game enough for this, and fortunately no common language was available. I decided to slip this place as soon as the weather permitted and to proceed to the smaller Sangboy Island, which lay close at hand on the far side of the island where I was sheltering. On Sangboy, I was looking forward to meeting again the Moro boy who had helped me to clean "Maring" at Karakol and the friendly people he had described to me.

I kept my lantern burning in the rigging and spent a most uncomfortable night. The idea of turning in among this wild-looking riff-raff was not attractive, but I was worn out and had to put my head down. I would have liked to imitate the famous Captain Slocum, who sprinkled drawing-pins all over his decks so that the cries of ill-intentioned Patagonians would waken him.

However, I need not have worried. Although I slept only three and a half hours, there was no sign of the vintas when I woke. My formal introduction into Moro society came the next day.

MORO COUNTRY

On 7th July, eight days after leaving Karakol, I left my anchorage to round the island, and sailed a couple of miles into the channel dividing North from Little Sangboy, anchoring some fifty yards from the beach. Although it was still early morning, a reception committee was already waiting for me. Sure enough, the unseen bush telegraph had been at work again. But there was something about the little group on shore that didn't feel right.

I had barely dropped the hook when a canoe load of grim-faced Moros all armed with kris and barongs, paddled alongside and climbed aboard without a word of explanation. There was something seriously wrong somewhere. One of them spoke English and informed me categorically that "The Chief" had come to inspect "Maring" and to search for firearms. "The Chief"—the Panglima, to give him his Moro title, was an elderly gentleman of even more uncompromising appearance than the rest. Apart from a scowl or two, he took not the slightest notice of me and immediately began clambering all over the boat. He and his henchmen searched "Maring" as thoroughly as Australian Customs Officers looking for opium. Meanwhile I stood around like a fool.

However, mindful of the customs of polite society, I thought of making the Panglima a pot of my precious China tea. This was not easy, with half a dozen men crawling all over the boat. But unwittingly I had struck the right note. Over the brew the great man relaxed somewhat and indicated to the interpreter that I might proceed to the protected anchorage farther up in the channel. He and his retainers stayed on board during the short sail in the morning

93

sunshine. When we arrived opposite the village, he left the boat with impressive dignity and without saying a single word.

There were more surprises to come. The interpreter stayed on board for a while and introduced himself as a Moro school-teacher, who had evacuated from Jolo Island some distance farther south when the Japanese had arrived there, and I got him to give me the explanation of my strange reception. As I suspected, the news of my sailing along the Peninsula had been common gossip ever since I struck Karakol. It was passed from vinta to vinta until it reached Sangboy and its Chief, the Panglima Sabdani, and when I had sheltered at North Sangboy the previous afternoon one of the vintas lying there had brought the news ahead of me. He also told me that, ferocious though these Moros looked, they were really quite harmless. They were sea gypsies belonging to the Samal tribe, itinerant fishermen of low caste.

Once again, the simple logic of the Moros had supplied the motive for my single-handed sailing. I had undoubtedly killed my fellow crew member or members so that I could have the boat and its profits to myself, and it had therefore been decided that I should be taken and put to the kris, a fate not uncommon for unbelievers who were foolish enough to blunder into isolated Moro islands alone and unarmed. To their minds, there was nothing wrong with the plan; on the contrary, it was their moral duty to carry it out. Did not the Koran command all Moslems to fight the unbelievers with fire and sword?

No sooner had the plan been agreed to than the young Moro from Karakol arrived in a trading vinta and told them that this crazy Americano—all white men were Americans round here—was really a bona fide single-hander. The Panglima was only half convinced, and in any event he was unwilling to abandon his plan of executing me, and he and his henchmen were actually in the process of making a vinta ready to come after me when I saved them the trouble by sailing round the point of the island.

Now I understood why the search had been so thorough. They were not only looking for firearms or other weapons, but also for evidence of a struggle, and for personal belongings other than my own. What the Chief saw must have convinced him that I was really quite harmless, only crazy.

My interpreter friend, who had a little education, professed himself horrified with this tale. But this did not prevent his telling it with much gusto, especially when it came to that part about killing me, "keel" he pronounced it. However, the episode seemed to have had a pleasant ending and I decided to go ashore.

North Sangboy was a small place, no bigger than an under-sized golf course and quite flat, one of the seven thousand one hundred and seven islands which—according to the Gazetteer—make up the territory of the Philippine Republic. There was a small coconut plantation, a swamp, a fringe of white coral beach and a reef around the island. There were thousands more like it, in this and in other parts of the Pacific.

When I came ashore by the few straggling huts near the beach, the atmosphere had changed violently—the word "violent" was to appear a lot in my diary and log during these next few months. There was no moderation about anything the Moros did or said. Their houses were ramshackle grass huts, miserable and primitive in the extreme, but the design, construction and ornamentation of their ships was of such beauty and perfection that they were works of art. They either hated their enemies to the point of killing without compunction, or they loved their friends and were fanatically loyal to them. The Middle Path was unknown to them.

Now the red carpet was rolled out. From being a bloody murderer, fit only to be killed, I became a hero and the mascot of the island. The Panglima took possession of me from the moment I stepped on shore and rarely left my side. The first thing he did was to present me with a small spear and scold me through the interpreter for being so stupid as to sail unarmed; and the next thing was to tell me that I looked like his eldest son who had been killed in one of the Moros' frequent battles with the Christian Filipinos on Mindanao. This was obviously intended to be a great compliment, although the Panglima spoke with his customary serious, almost threatening expression. In fact, I don't remember ever seeing him smile—but there was no doubt of his good will. He next paraded me around the island with our school-teacher-interpreter tagging along astern.

Sangboy was not much of a place. The Japanese occupation had thoroughly disorganized the life of the people, and most of them had evacuated to Mindanao, where they could hide more easily. In normal times they made their living by trading and, to a lesser extent, by fishing, but with the disruption of inter-island traffic they had been hard hit. For their staple food, they depended on rice, and little was now reaching them; so they lived mainly on bread baked with cassava flour, a meal ground from a tuberous root cultivated throughout the southern Philippines. The children were naked and covered with ulcers and scabs which were beset with swarms of flies.

On my first day, the Panglima took me to pay a courtesy visit to the house of a rival chief, mysteriously called the Maharadja Ticaul. The Maharadja invited us to a meal of rice and fish and showed me some beautiful kris and barongs inlaid with silver and copper. The kris is a short sword with a wavy blade, and the barong is a refined form of Filipino bolo, both are murderous weapons. These were works of great craftsmanship; the scabbards were inlaid with mother-of-pearl in patterns which clearly showed Arabic influence. Their ships and their swords, these were the things the Moros loved best.

The people on Sangboy lived in great fear of "mundos", the Moro pirates whose business had suddenly boomed when the Philippine administration ceased to function. The Japanese were not wise to the tricks of the trade which these men had pursued for many centuries—this was hardly surprising, since, although the Spaniards and Americans had been trying to stop piracy for the last three centuries, it had never been quite stamped out. The "mundos" often shifted their hideouts among the hundreds of islands in the Sulu Group, many of which were uninhabited, and from each new base they would pounce on traders and plunder villages. They had excellent mobility with their fast vintas, and they could concentrate fleets of forty to fifty vintas quickly to achieve surprise and numerical superiority in attack. When the deed was done, or when danger threatened, they could disperse just as quickly. A nest of mundos had been reported on Pilas Island, twenty-five miles south-west of Sangboy, and the previous night there had been some robbing and killing on Great Sangboy Island across the channel—while I had been anchored off-shore!

During our meal with the Maharadja Ticaul, the Panglima had been seized with an idea, and on our way back to the main part of the village he informed me through the interpreter of his decision. Because he admired the way I sailed alone, he said, and because I looked so much like his son who had been a famous fighter, he had decided to adopt me as his son. He attached great importance to the proposed relationship and explained that such an adoption was sanctioned by the tribal and religious laws of the Moros.

I was most apprehensive about the whole idea. What rights would he consider he had over me? How would my new status affect my freedom to continue my voyage? However, with the Panglima glowing with pride and benevolence, this was not the time to show reluctance or to ask awkward questions, and I therefore accepted the honour subject to one condition: that I should not have to change

97

my religion. After a minute's thought he accepted my condition and announced that the official ceremony would take place a few days later, adding that he wished to keep me on the island, where I would be safe from the Japanese for the duration of the war. I let it go for the moment.

Next, when we reached the open space in the centre of the village, I was asked if I would like my hair cut. As there had not been an opportunity to have it done for months and I felt decidedly thick on top, this seemed an excellent idea. Only after I had agreed did I realize that this "haircut" was to be a formal affair and a step in the process that was to make me a synthetic Moro. I was led to a stool in the centre of a ring of villagers assembled for the occasion and then subjected to the torture of having my head shaved with a blunt knife and without soap. With all those stern faces watching me and all those shaven heads indicating that my "haircut" was quite a normal procedure, I had to keep any protests or yelps under strong control and, in fairness to the barber, I must add that I emerged from this ordeal with fewer cuts than I believed possible, and certainly I felt a good deal cooler.

I had never worn a hat, but now with my shaven poll I needed protection against the midday sun. The Panglima had already thought of that and presented me with an ornate Moro hat. It was shaped like a cone and was made of several layers of nipah palm leaves held together with rattan strips woven into a pattern of light and dark colours. I was truly grateful for the gift. Not only would I now look like a Moro from a distance at sea, but the hat was entirely water-tight. It was the perfect sun helmet.

I wished very much that I still had my camera. I wanted to have some documentary proof that all these unlikely things did actually happen. Throughout my stay in Moro country I rarely lost the feeling that I was in some sort of fairyland and that no one would believe me when I came to tell about it afterwards.

98

Although I was invited by the Panglima to stay in his house, I decided to remain on board. There had been one attempt at robbery already. Of all people, the youth who had helped me at Karakol had stolen my watch and assorted clothing. The watch was returned by other natives who had seen him.

"Maring" had to be kept seaworthy. Her bottom had again become fouled—the growth was incredibly quick here—and I careened her at low tide. Also I was able to barter a quantity of excellent Jolo hemp rope in exchange for wet sugar. This stroke of luck came in the nick of time, and I immediately renewed all sheets, halliards and lanyards.

But the sail was a heartbreaking sight. It was almost impossible to repair it. When I took it off the spars and laid it out on the flat ground ashore, the fabric had the feeling of tenderness which usually precedes total disintegration. I was able to mend the worst tears, but did not dare do much patching because the cloth could barely take the stitches. A new sail was out of the question. I had no cash, and the Moros were themselves desperately struggling to keep their own fleets in order; so I did what I could, but I could not hope that these sails would take me much farther.

Disturbing news now came in. Japanese patrols were reported all around these islands, operating out of Zamboanga —barely thirty miles from Sangboy—and from Basilan Island to the South of the peninsula. It was regarded as a wonder that I had not fallen in with them more often. They had several small launches and had worked out a regular pattern of sea patrols in their search for arms smugglers, for escaping white men and Moro pirates. This news made necessary a detour of fifty miles. I decided to sail due west for about twenty-five miles, and then turn south-east to pass midway between Basilan and Jolo into the Celebes Sea.

It was not easy to convince the Panglima that I must leave him and expose myself to the fatal risk of encountering Japanese patrols, not to mention Moro "mundos" when he was anxious to have me stay on Sangboy and take my place as his adopted son, and I could see the possibility of a very ugly situation when I had to show him that my mind was made up.

Then Moro sailors from the Tawi-Tawi islands sailed in to Sangboy, and my plans changed again.

On 9th July, two days after my arrival, I wrote in my diary:

"Returning to this diary today with a heavy heart, for I must now face the possibility of being delayed for three more months until the south-west monsoon abates and north winds set in. This is not a sudden decision. Ever since watching the boat sail to windward in only moderately heavy weather in the opening between Negros and Mindanao, I have become convinced of the impossibility of making appreciable progress if I should have to tack for longer distances, especially with the present sails which have deteriorated beyond hope of effective repair during the two hundred and fifty mile trip so far.

"This morning, sailors from the Tawi-Tawi islands, reputedly the most competent mariners amongst the sea-minded Moros, passed here and gave the first expert advice I have had, gathered from their experience of long trips as far S.E. as New Guinea and S. to Timor. They say winds will be around S. all the way down and stronger in S. latitudes, that I will not reach my destination in five months, that I need two suits of sails. Exaggerated, but I can draw my own conclusions—approximately the same. From October onwards, they think, it would be easy, with a fair wind blowing all the way. Their story tallies approximately with the scanty information in the Philippine Pilot on the same topic.

"Determination and will power can accomplish much but can hardly change the S.W. monsoon or mend a rotted sail.

"Problems connected with delay are many, mainly concerned with hideout, supply and finance. Thinking
several schemes over."

At first the idea of hanging around for three more months
was unbearable and I had moments of despair and near
panic; it would be Santa Barbara and Iloilo all over again.
But that mood didn't last long. I had to take my impatience
in hand and accept the fact. What I had suspected had been
confirmed by experienced sailors: it would be madness to go
on trying to sail south against the prevailing wind. The
south-west monsoon was now firmly established and my
sail would have flown out of the bolt-ropes before I had even
reached the northernmost of the Moluccas. I sat on deck and
felt sorry for myself. Some naked brown children were
playing with a coconut shell in the shallow water. I had
rigged a sun awning over the hatch and was cooled by a
steady wind—but the wind came from the south.

As soon as he heard my new decision, the Panglima Sabdani had the solution to all my problems. I was to stay in
Sangboy. The boat could be hidden in any one of the
hundreds of mangrove lagoons, he said, or on nearby
islands, many of which were not shown on any but Admiralty charts. I was to stay as his guest, he needed no payment. He swore he would rather let himself be killed than
betray my hiding-place to Japanese patrols or Quisling
police. The interpreter did overtime that day. The old man
was completely sincere, and I loved him for it.

He even held out more attractive inducements. There
would be women, I was to be married off to one or more of
his subjects. All of a sudden I felt as if I were seeing an old
film again, years afterwards. Where had I heard this before?
Of course, I had read it in one of the books by Alan Villiers.
Exactly the same thing had happened to him in this neigh-
bourhood some years before. If I remembered rightly, they
went a little farther with him and actually put girls under his

mosquito net at night. I was never a woman-hater, but there is a time and a place for everything and it was not here. Besides, the lovelies here were angular, and they chewed betel-nut.

I had to be very diplomatic in warding off Sabdani's insistence. If it had crossed his mind he could easily have used force instead of persuasion. Accepting his offer to hide me was out of the question, although it was genuinely meant and I did not doubt that the rest of the islanders would be behind him. But there were many traitors about. A Moro would do a lot for a wrist-watch. For firearms, many would have cheerfully killed their grandmothers, and it would not take the Japanese long to find this out.

I decided that my only chance of keeping out of the way of the Japanese was on Mindanao, second-biggest island of the Philippine Archipelago and largely unexplored. There were hundreds of miles of forbidding, roadless coastline where it should be possible to spend three months, and I might even be able to use my only asset, "Maring", to earn my keep and get a new sail before I set out again.

It was difficult to refuse the islanders' hospitality, but it had to be done. Their eagerness to keep me was puzzling. What were their motives? Was it genuine hospitality and anxiety for my fate? Or was it curiosity and a wish to possess something exotic and strange for a while? I never found out the exact answer, and they could probably not have given it to me. I preferred to think that hospitality was their main reason, and I was probably right.

The ceremony of my adoption into Sabdani's household took place on 11th July, the fourth day of my stay. As with ceremonies all over the world, a big meal was a part of it. Everyone was dressed in their most vividly contrasting trousers and blouses, all wearing colourful headcloths. The men were fully armed with their kris. The women wore neat sarongs and stayed in the background.

The ritual came first. It took place in the Panglima Sab-

THE MAP (*scale* 1: 12,500,000), TAKEN FROM A DUTCH ATLAS, WHICH SERVED AS THE MASTER CHART FOR ALL NAVIGATION WORKSHEETS

Sketch of "MARING"
Overall Length : 24 feet.
Beam   7', 6"
Draft   2' , 3"

SKETCH OF "MARING"

"KAKUGAN"

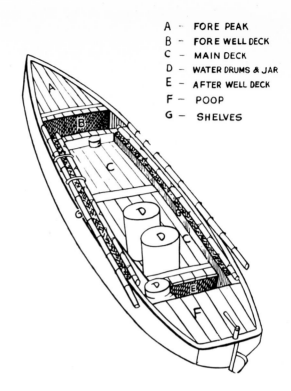

A - FORE PEAK
B - FORE WELL DECK
C - MAIN DECK
D - WATER DRUMS & JAR
E - AFTER WELL DECK
F - POOP
G - SHELVES

A - MAIN SL
B - GUY LINES
C - HALLIARD AND BACKSTAY
D - SHROUDS
E - SHEET
F - MAST

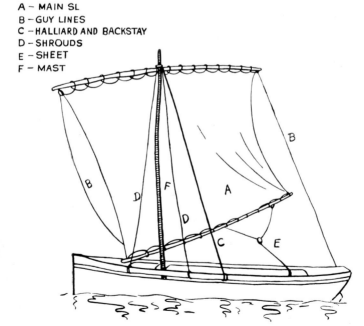

SKETCHES SHOWING THE LAY-OUT AND RIG OF "KAKUGAN"

LIEUTENANT FRANK YOUNG, D.S.C. (U.S.A.)

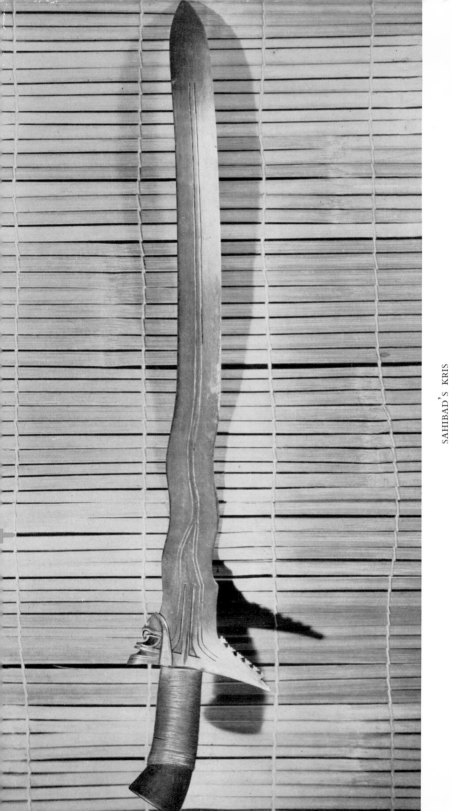

SAHIBAD'S KRIS

With which the author was to have been beheaded

"KAKUGAN'S" CREW

A photograph taken on the day "Kakugan" reached South Goulburn Mission Station.
(*Left to right*) Lieut. Young, the author, Manguma, Ajijohn, Sabdal, Sahibad, Dalil, and Ali. Note "Bird" in the foreground.

THE AFTER GUARD

(*Left to right*) Lieut. Young, the author, Sahibad

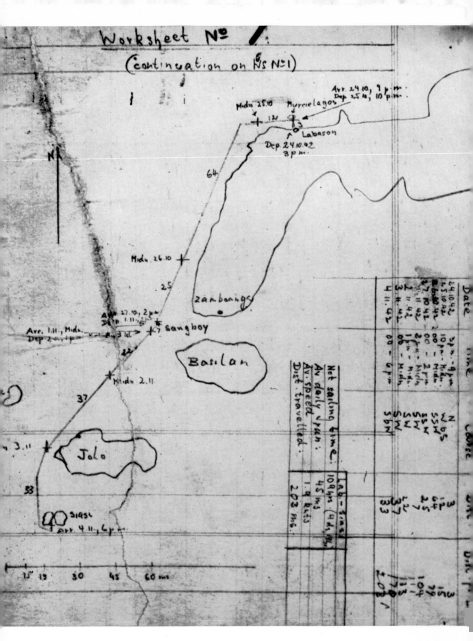

NAVIGATION WORKSHEET NO. I

Section Labason to Siasi

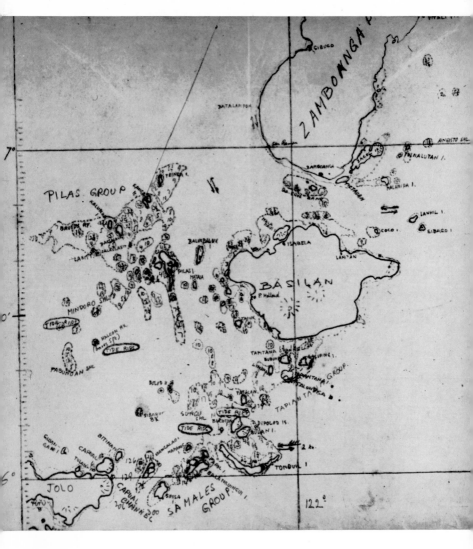

PENCILLED CHART .

Copied from Admiralty Chart, showing Zamboanga and adjacent Waters

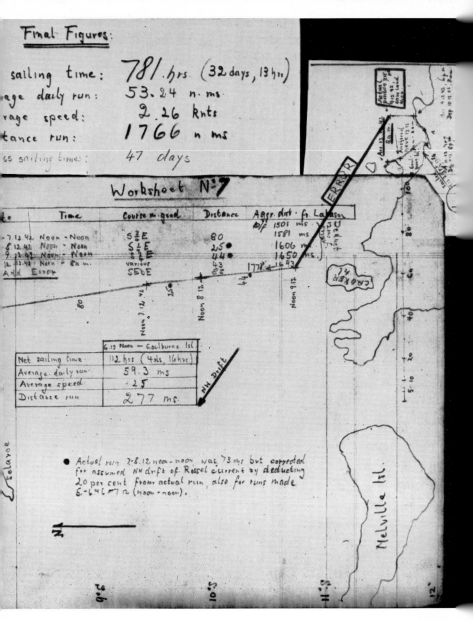

Final Figures:

sailing time: **781** hrs (32 days, 13 hrs)

rage daily run: 53.24 n. ms.

rage speed: 2.26 knts

tance run: 1766 n ms

ss sailing time: 47 days

Worksheet N° 7

te	Time	Course & speed	Distance	Aggr. dist. fr. Labasos
7.12.42 Noon - Noon		S¾E	80	b/f 1501 ms
8.12.42 Noon - Noon		S¼E	25	1581 ms
9.12.42 Noon - Noon		S¼E	44	1606 ms
12.12.42 Noon - 8 a.m.		various	43	1650 ms.
Add Error		S5°E	65	1778 — 1693

	6.12 Noon — Goulburne Isl.
Net sailing time:	112 hrs (4 dys, 16 hrs)
Average daily run:	59.3 ms
Average speed:	.25
Distance run	277 ms.

• Actual run 7-8.12 noon-noon was 73 ms but corrected
for assumed NW drift of Rossel current by deducting
20 per cent from actual run, also for runs made
5-6 & 6-7 12 (noon-noon).

NAVIGATION WORKSHEET NO. VII
Section E. of Jamdena to South Goulburn Island (off Australian mainland)

PENCILLED CHART
Copied from Admiralty Index Chart, showing Ceram and Arafura Seas

dani's house. Sabdani and I sat opposite each other on mats, and between us there was an ornate brass tray with plates of hard-boiled eggs and coffee. To one side, sat the Hadji, who had been to Mecca and wore his green turban. This old gentleman did duty as the local Moslem priest, and he said a lot of prayers, of which I could understand nothing except the occasional mention of Allah. Then Sabdani and I peeled our eggs, exchanged them and ate. Coffee followed, the Hadji said some more prayers, in which the rest of the islanders, who were sitting in a large circle around us, joined. Sabdani was quite moved and kept telling me how happy he was that now I was the son to take the place of the one killed.

Then came the feast. Rice, chicken, eggs and more coffee. We tried to make ourselves understood without the interpreter, but the conversation was limited. Sabdani spoke Moro and Tagalog, with a few Spanish words. But I had only a very few words in those languages and his English was about the same. Nevertheless, we managed to understand each other on a few limited topics. At least a hundred times, one of us said "Soldado nippon hombre malo", to which the other was expected to make vigorous grunts and noises of affirmation. Japanese soldiers were bad men. The weather was similarly treated. It was all very jolly.

Then I was formally introduced to the rest of my family. They were my two black-toothed foster mothers and nine children of assorted sizes and sexes. Not being wealthy, Sabdani could afford only two wives.

At last the Panglima and I reached a compromise regarding my future movements. I now accepted his veto on going south and promised, if it should be possible, to return to Sangboy in October, when I intended to make a fresh start. He in turn gave up trying to keep me on the island and gave me directions how to reach places along the Zamboanga Peninsula where white men were reported to be living. This meant that I would have to retrace my course for about eighty miles.

On the following day, after five days on Sangboy, I said goodbye to the Panglima Sabdani. The ship was made ready for sea and I turned north with the sheets free.

I lost my disappointment in the pure joy of watching "Maring" sail. Now that we had the wind behind us she made a good job of it, and during the first twenty-four hours after leaving Sangboy we sailed forty-five miles. During that night we crossed the steamer lane to Zamboanga un-molested.

Near the Zamboanga coast in the morning, I was be-calmed. There was quite a bit of life under the seas close to the shore. I saw a large turtle, his back all grown with barnacles. He sounded as I approached. Sea snakes un-dulated through the water quite near the surface. They were ugly yellow-black mottled monsters in all sizes. Not for the gold of India would I have swum in those waters.

I worked my way northward now, losing a day in a wild-goose chase after an American reported to be living in Sibuko Bay village. I sailed close in-shore, but found only a deserted coconut grove, some dilapidated shacks and a few fishermen.

"Maring" gave no trouble except for her poor sails. Looking up at them, I used to wonder anxiously if they would last until Guimaras, if I could not find a hiding-place on Mindanao. The canvas was beyond mending, and new holes appeared every day. I had not sailed in the tropics be-fore, and found it hard to understand that deterioration could spread so rapidly. To get a new set of sails was my main worry now, and it was almost as big a problem as getting my boat had been.

Except for her sails, "Maring" made me happy. I had staying in her down to a fine art, losing little way in the process. I would pay off first, and then, with some speed, round through the wind before she had time to stop her fat nose half-way through. She handled easily and would have been ideal for single-handed sailing if she had had two headsails instead of one. I developed quite an affection for the little unassuming ship with her tubby bows and her top-sides of unpainted wood gone grey with years of exposure.

I was now searching for a place called Labason in Sindan-gan Bay, where, according to Sabdani, an American was living. I had no detailed chart of Mindanao waters, but on Sangboy they had given me landmarks and I hoped for the best.

Anxious to find a hole to hide in for the next few months, I sailed during the night again. On 15th July I noted in my log:

"Weary after sailing all night. 'Starry Splendour of the tropics' velvety sky' as they say in the books, is all right with six hours sleep behind or before you, but I find night sailing very taxing and all I can do is to keep awake and on my course. After working ship all day, five hours sleep is my minimum, my body just goes on strike. Am still soft and envy sturdy captains who can keep the bridge for forty-eight hours on end.

"Now the steep headlands of Coronado Point are in view, gaining a good offing to double it."

On 16th July I found Labason without difficulty and anchored in front of the Chinese trader's store. A European came aboard and introduced himself as Horace Friend, manager of one of the local rice mills. The mysterious bush telegraph had done its work again; Friend knew all about me. After I had explained my situation, he invited me to stay at Labason with the same disarming matter-of-course hospitality which I had encountered so often among people living beyond the borders of city civilization.

I conned "Maring" into the river, across a bar which her draft could only just clear, then I took my gear out of her. She had been a faithful boat and I was confident I could trust her to see me through whatever lay ahead.

IV. WAITING FOR THE MONSOON

LABASON

THE problem of how to live during the next three months was solved with unexpected speed. "Maring" was chartered to Chia, one of the Chinese traders whom Friend advised me was reliable. By verbal contract he was to have exclusive use of my boat until 15th October. In consideration of this, Chia was to pay for my board at Friend's house and for my tobacco. "Maring" was to be returned to me intact with a new set of sails, and with provisions on the same scale as when I first left Guimaras. Two hundred pieces of dried fish were to be added. Chia said he might give me some cash in addition if trading profits warranted it.

It was a strange thought, being kept by a sailing-boat. But the bargain was completely satisfactory, it covered exactly what I needed. There was no agreement on paper, not that that would have been worth much, anyway. I took a good look at Chia and liked him. A very wide-awake young man. Still, I disliked intensely the idea of trusting all I had to a stranger.

I watched while my boat was being taken over. The firewood was unloaded and the water drum removed. Chia wasted no time. Three days later "Maring" sailed for a port on Negros with a crew of four and a cargo of thirty-five sacks of rice. And my prayers went with the little boat as she left the bay. If anything happened to her, that would be the end of my plans. Although I never gave up hope of finding a shipmate, I had been disappointed so often that I could only count on myself, and none of the boats built or sailed

106

in the Mindanao area were possible for a single-handed sailing voyage.

Mr. Horace Friend was well named. He opened his house to me and I became one of the family. He himself was a Filipino citizen born in the islands, his wife was a Filipino girl from the Visayas and she was kindness itself to me. The running of their house was easy and free, and Mr. Friend's work at the rice mill left ample time for eating and drinking and gossiping. Early in the afternoon the mahjong tokens would come out, and late at night I often went to sleep in my room on the first floor, to the clicking noise of the stones. When Chia and other friends came in, the sessions would go on into the early morning by the light of a couple of hurricane lanterns hanging from the ceiling. I never played mahjong with them, because I was hopeless at games. Moreover, they were mainly talking in Tagalog, which I could not understand, and, finally, they played for money and I had none.

At first my inactivity didn't worry me. The south-west monsoon brought rain nearly every day and I slept a lot— the trip in "Maring" had taken more out of me than I had realized. My host lived on the edge of the town, on slightly higher ground near some palm groves; on the cool, clear, moonlit nights after the rain the air was fresh with the fragrance of strange blossoms, and in the mangrove swamps by the river a million crickets and mosquitoes started their evening concert. These were peaceful surroundings for the day's last pipe and a note scribbled in my diary.

So far as any danger from the Japanese went, for the moment I had nothing to fear. Labason was a small town on a narrow coastal plain in Sindangan Bay, protected on the south and west by high mountains covered with trackless jungle. To the north-east lay Sindangan, another small town, from which warning would come quickly at the approach of a Japanese shore patrol. From seaward, watching posts on both headlands would give warning of any patrol boats coming into the area. But this was hardly necessary. The only people who had fuel to run motor boats were the Japanese, and whenever the noise of an engine was heard, it was a foregone conclusion that a patrol or raiding party from the garrison at Zamboanga was on the way. To make things even more secure, the foreshore was shallow, so that a launch had to anchor well out and ferry passengers ashore by canoe or sailing-boat.

Labason had its own guerilla force of about two hundred men. They were called the Volunteer Guards and were commanded by a Filipino, Lieutenant Melicor. They were clad in blue denim, the fatigue uniform of the Philippine Army, and only a few were armed with rifles—about one in seven—and the rest had "paltiks", locally made shotguns which were more dangerous to the firer than the target. The boys could usually be seen lounging around the bazaar, and while I stayed at Labason I did not see them train or commit any war-like acts against the Japanese. On the contrary, whenever there was report of an approaching enemy patrol, the guerilla force would be conveniently "concentrated" in the hills a long way off. I had a lot of pleasant talks with Lieutenant Melicor, but I could never find out anything about the Guard's activities, except what many people in town told me privately. They were more afraid of their own guerillas than they were of the Japanese. The Japanese took only their rice, their fuel and a chicken here and there, but the guerillas took all that and, in addition, regularly levied large contributions for the permanent support of the unit.

Later on guerilla warfare became properly organized in the Philippines, but as I saw it then, the term covered everything from splendid and devoted service to sheer banditry.

When I first reached Labason the Japanese had not yet been there, but a week later four policemen in Japanese pay arrived from Sindangan to hunt for hidden whites and to confiscate rice and motor fuel. There was no panic at all,

I simply stayed in Friend's house all day. The Japanese agents were entertained by Chia and by Friend himself. They were kept busy playing mahjong and won considerable amounts from Chia, which only went to show what fine diplomats the Chinese were.

After the scare was over, I suggested to Friend that my stay with him might compromise him and endanger his family's safety. He discounted my fears and wouldn't hear of my leaving his home. I hoped that my having been there would not harm him later.

Soon afterwards the Japanese themselves came. We had our usual warnings, and I spent a week-end in hiding among the friendly hill people in the mountains. The town looked peaceful enough from my vantage point. The guerillas had disappeared as usual, and the houses were flying home-made little Rising Sun flags. The Japanese grabbed all available rice and generally raised hell, but did not actually shoot the place up. Everybody was relieved when they left and I strolled leisurely down the mountain path as their launch chugged out of the bay.

After that visit, the Japanese and their Filipino hatchet-men left Labason alone for many weeks. The sea was generally too rough and the narrow road from Sindangan became a quagmire.

The south-west monsoon was now really here. Day after day it blew as strongly as it ever did in these latitudes. We were well into the rainy season, the dirt paths of the town became puddles and streams, and inside the houses there was much shuffling about of enamel basins and other containers to catch the water from the leaking nipah roofs. On the occasional sunny days the whole place steamed and we steamed with it.

Now and then news came in from "Maring". Sometimes she was weatherbound in this port or that, but she was kept fairly well at work, and Chia was satisfied with the profits.

The Friends were kindness itself and treated me as one of the household. Meals were taken whenever they felt like it, sometimes I was woken in the middle of the night when the fishermen had come in with a good catch. Everybody drank a lot of tuba, that horrible coconut-palm wine, and mahjong continued to be the ruling passion. It was a vice for many who could not afford to play, and when they got into debt they mortgaged everything they owned, including next year's rice crop. One day Chia gambled away his whole store—but fortunately not "Maring". He bounced back immediately, and next morning had started trading with a few fish again. He got up while everybody slept and secured a corner on the market for that day. No doubt he would have his store back before long. The people took these things very calmly.

I went to Mass with my hosts one Sunday morning. They were devout Catholics, like most Filipinos. The House of God here was a board shack and the service was said in a mixture of Latin and Spanish, and the sermon was given in Visayan. The attendance was startling: thirty-five women and girls and six men.

With Friend, I went to weddings and to other native festivities. After a good win at mahjong Chia gave us a colossal Chinese feast, which included a tasty dish of sharks' fins and pickled pork. Then Mrs. Friend had a baby and there was another celebration. The child arrived in the morning, but this did not prevent Mrs. Friend from cooking the evening rice.

I made many acquaintances among the locals, who treated me as one of themselves after a while, and I got a fascinating insight into local politics. Labason was really a frontier town. There were a few rice mills where the farmers from surrounding districts delivered their grain, a school, a dispensary and a small municipio, but the real centre of the town was the bazaar, an unmade street with stalls on both sides where the Chinese did their trading.

This was the hub of the place and the most important news exchange.

The native tribes, who were gentle and timid and comparatively small in number, had been pushed back into the hills by the arrival of more advanced and vigorous colonists from other islands—this was a pattern of development that had taken place all over the Pacific. On this part of the coast, the invasion was a recent one. Most of the settlers were Visayans, Christian Filipinos from the thickly populated island of Panay, and had been in the area for less than a generation. There was land enough for all, and these two races could have lived together peacefully enough if it had not been for the simultaneous settlement of Moslem Moros from the south. The fatal combination of economic and religious rivalry which resulted had led to a feud of long standing. At times this was smoothed over, and at other times deteriorated into open bloodshed, and although everything appeared peaceful for the moment, tension was always there and war conditions intensified it.

Labason was almost entirely populated by Christian Filipinos, and only a few Moros with good records were tolerated there, although many more Moros held title deeds to rice lands and naturally cherished a tailor-made grudge. In nearby Quipit the situation was reversed, the Moros ruled it. Both towns continually threatened to eat each other, and it was a regular war within a war, with Labason one of the chief battle-grounds. When I arrived, Labason was leading Quipit one up in this game, having just recently pounced on a number of Moros and executed them for being pro-Japanese. Calling one another "pro-Japanese" became the greatest swear word of all and a heaven-sent excuse—if they needed it—for further quarrels and fights.

The *real* war in that part of Mindanao was between Christian and Moslems and I, having come there from Moro country, listened fascinated but refrained from comment.

Outwardly life continued to be paradisaical, with the added advantage that there was no Eve. I ate, I swam, I loafed and I read the same old magazines over and over again, but inevitably, in spite of the Friends' kindness, with returning energy I became bored and impatient. I was going through the same frustration I had endured in Iloilo, only here I knew that there was a time limit. In mid-October, the monsoon would set in and I would have "Maring" back again. But that was more than two months away.

I became restless and went for walks, amusing myself watching the monkeys and listening to the many parrots, which I could seldom see. They were up in the high roof of the forest, hidden by lower branches and vines and tree-trunks.

Later I asked myself why I did not spend my time better. I wasn't worried about the Japanese finding me, I was paying my way—or my boat was paying it for me—and I had three months to relax in. I ought to have explored the interior a bit, or collected butterflies or studied the love life of ants. I could have watched cock-fights, or learned the proper stance for barong and kris fighting.

But I did none of these things. I could think only of "Maring" and of the forthcoming voyage. All other thoughts and activities were incidental to the main purpose. The only things I enjoyed were looking around me and talking to the many interesting new people I met. For three weeks I did not even write in my diary.

The lack of reliable news from the outside world was tantalizing. We had some sort of a radio, but it would not work. We tried desperately to get it going with the help of a run-down motor-car battery, which we attempted to charge with a small dynamo in the Chinese rice mill, but it never worked. Everybody was rumoured to be capturing everything. Two-thirds of Germany had been taken by Russia, the Americans had landed on Formosa, Chinese and Dutch forces had reoccupied Singapore, Hong Kong, Amoy and Nanking. The Japanese had landed half a million troops in Alaska. . . . The only credible story concerned the appearance of American submarines outside Zamboanga. These were described in unmistakable detail by arrivals from that part of the island.

If only October were here! I was bored stiff.

I had been in Labason a month before something happened which snapped me out of my indolence. It was on 18th August that a native clergyman, who had been visiting the hiding-place of a group of American missionaries, returned to the town. He had told them of me and there was a chance of a shipmate among them, and he brought from them an invitation to visit their camp.

The prospect of a new diversion, as well as finding a sailing companion, was very welcome, and I immediately made arrangements to sail the following day, weather permitting, with a native trader who was bound south along the coast. I took only a few belongings and left the rest of my gear, including my navigation instruments, in Friend's care.

"FOREST GLEN"

Trader Alvarez put me off at the little coastal village of Malayal, which lay at the foot of steep heavily wooded mountains some sixty miles to the north of Zamboanga. He handed me over to waiting guides, promised to meet me in the same place in a week's time and had barely reached his boat again before we plunged into the twilight of the jungle.

This was my first introduction to the interior of a tropical rain forest. We began climbing up through a deep valley along a clear stream, jumping over boulders, clambering around the stumps of ancient trees and occasionally trying to walk along slippery fallen trunks. Now and then a shaft of sunlight would penetrate the canopy overhead and strike through the moisture-laden air to light up a spot of clear green water bordered with moss-covered rocks, but only by bending one's head right back could one see small patches of sky through the dark-green roof of leafy branches, orchids and tree parasites. Occasionally a troop of monkeys playing around the higher branches startled the hornbills into protesting shrieks, crickets were hard at their scraping, and when the cicadas joined in at midday the noise was deafening. As we passed, lizards of all shapes and colours scuttled away, and sometimes a snake slithered out of sight.

After two or three back-breaking miles we came to a slight bend in the steep valley, where a warning post had been set up some distance below the camp. Here one of the missionaries was waiting to greet me. He dismissed the guides and led me farther up until we rounded another bend and came into full view of the camp, which had been built on a slope only a little less steep than the rest of the valley.

All undergrowth had been cleared from a considerable site beneath the huge trees, and among them stood neat houses, a kitchen, a school and a church, all made of timber and nipah palm. This was the jungle hideout of twenty-nine men, women and children of the Christian and Missionary Alliance in the Philippine Islands. They called their retreat "Forest Glen".

I was made welcome by the Chairman and his wife, the Reverend and Mrs. Gulbranson, who showed me round and told me the history of the camp.

These missionaries had all worked in different parts of southern Mindanao for many years, some of them for a lifetime, and they knew the country intimately and loved it as their home. When Japan came into the War they were called from their outlying stations to Zamboanga. A suitable hiding-place had been reconnoitred in January and was occupied in March, before the Japanese landings took place. Of their total number, only sixteen were adults, and of these, two were quite elderly; another man and woman were in-

capable of hard physical work. What the remaining dozen
had accomplished in barely six months was astonishing.
Their little settlement in the forest looked like an illustration
for Hansel and Gretel out of a children's book.

"Forest Glen" was a place of order and beauty compared
to the rough and dilapidated frontier settlements which
passed for villages elsewhere on the Zamboanga coast. The
place was well laid out and spotlessly clean and tidy. The
houses were neat, and it was easy to see that tidy American
housewives were living in them. Some had curtains at the
windows, and the paths between the buildings were
bordered with stones. There was a communal kitchen and a
separate building which served as dining and assembly hall.
At the upper end of the slope was the school house, and
farther up a little outcropping on the side of the mountain
slope had been converted into a shelter with benches and a
table. This hummock was called "Snake Hill" because of
the many snakes that had been seen there. Two paths leading to it had been neatly cleared and steps cut.

Their garden was the most amazing feat of all. About
half a mile from "Forest Glen" a site of three acres had been
cleared for a garden, as small food-producing tracts were
called hereabouts. The labour must have been colossal.
Huge trees had been felled, the underbrush cut away and the
area fired, leaving charred logs and ash to cover the ground.
They had planted corn and sweet potatoes from seeds presented to them by friendly natives. Things grew quickly so
near the equator, and when I arrived they had already har-
vested their first crop and the second was well on the way.

The monkeys liked the garden too, and they and the
missionaries had a standing fight. The monkeys used cunning, the missionaries fought a losing battle with sticks and
stones. The monkeys hunted in troops, and we used to
observe them for hours from a watch-tower which had been
placed in the centre of the garden in the hope of keeping
them away.

One monkey would make a colossal fuss and noise in one corner of the plot, and the attention of the watchers would be concentrated on him. At the same time, twenty or thirty of the brutes would raid the extreme opposite end of the field without making any noise at all. By the time we had discovered the main party it was too late, they ran away triumphant, carrying ears of corn, and the next day they would try a completely different plan. Years later, at army staff schools, I was to be introduced to the laudable military maxim: "Mislead, Mystify and Deceive." The Mindanao monkeys knew it all by heart. They became so destructive that a dawn-to-dusk watch had to be kept. The Reverend Christie who had something wrong with his legs and could not take part in the daily hard labour of the camp, was made Monkey-Hunter-in-Chief. He was carried to the watch-tower and stayed there for many hours, with a good supply of stones by his side.

There were less-picturesque nuisances than monkeys. One day when I was on a working party at the edge of the garden, I leaned my hand on a tree-stump. There was something black there, and when I looked again the biggest scorpion in creation stared me in the face. He was at least three inches long. Snakes were everywhere, I had never seen so many, and huge bull-ants.

I was quartered in a hammock in the school, a half-open nipah-covered shed, high up, close to the narrow and overgrown tracks which led into the farther interior. For a while I could not sleep well. Forest life was quite different from anything I had been used to until then. I had a feeling of being trapped, of oppression. Things went bump in the night, animal cries, a flying fox or only a falling branch.

I had come to find a shipmate here, but I was unlucky. The gentleman who had considered coming along was the only non-missionary member of the camp. Before the Japanese invasion he had been in charge of a "Gospel Ship", a little vessel belonging to another missionary society which worked along the Mindanao coast. He was an elderly man and asked me a lot of questions about "Maring" and about my navigation. Apparently he did not like what he heard and saw, and decided against joining me, but he was most helpful and gave me much valuable local advice. Most important, he allowed me to copy three of the maps in his possession; they were Admiralty Index Charts which showed the ten-fathom line and the height of the islands in the area through which I intended to pass. Knowing the height of many of these smaller islands would help me to recognize my landfalls and, by taking bearings on them, would enable me to fix positions more accurately. It took me several days to copy them with carbon on sheets of white paper.

The missionaries themselves were either too old to come along or they had families. One of the younger men gave the idea some thought for a while, but eventually he too had to decline. He could not possibly leave his wife and small son alone in that camp.

I arrived in the camp late in August and originally planned to stay a week. But the trader who had promised to call on his way back to Labason did not show up. I worried about the safety of "Maring" and wondered whether they were looking after her, but except for this, there was no hurry for my return; the monsoon would be blowing the wrong way for many weeks yet. The missionaries did not appear anxious to get rid of me, and I liked being with them. In the end I stayed seven weeks.

Apart from an occasional afternoon tea with an Anglican minister in Japan, I had not come in contact much with the clergy in the Far East. Of missionaries I knew nothing. In the big port cities of Shanghai, Kobe and Yokohama, missionaries were the butts of many jokes. Many an evening in the Club was enlivened with the latest story about their supposed doings. The jokes were never vicious, but they were thoughtless in a casual sort of way. After my stay in

"Forest Glen" I don't think I ever laughed at a joke about missionaries again.

Of course missionaries are not angels. They make mistakes, and some are over-zealous in trying to force their particular brand of salvation on natives who do not want it. Some no doubt are bigoted, mean and narrow-minded, and nearly all of them are quixotic. It is not really possible to generalize.

The missionaries I met here in the forest were quite different. Probably, in their peacetime stations, they had been as individualistic and troublesome as most of us are. But the common danger had made them rise above themselves. Coming to the camp, I felt at once an unmistakable spirit of harmony and common purpose. There seemed to be no need for their chairman, the Reverend Gulbranson, to exercise any authority at all. His main duties were to ration their limited stores, such as kerosene and coconut oil.

Everyone worked. Occasionally native Christians in the area gave them some help, but on the whole the missionaries conducted the camp unaided. The children attended school, the Reverend Christie was Headmaster and had a regular staff, and Miss Bohleen was in charge of the kindergarten. They even had a school bell made out of a hollow bamboo log. As most of the missionaries were professional teachers, the children received as good an education in the camp as they would have got in their own homes.

As if the missionaries did not have enough to do trying to keep themselves alive, they still carried out work among the surrounding natives. These were of the gentle Subano tribe, an indigenous race which had been pushed back into the hills by the immigration of Moros and Filipinos. They were simple folk and helped the missionaries all they could. There was no traitor among them. The missionaries settled their quarrels, performed their marriage ceremonies and gave medical advice and treatment.

I occasionally accompanied the missionaries on these trips

to small native settlements farther inland. The going was hard and kept them in condition. On one occasion it took us more than five hours each way to travel a distance of three miles as the crow flies—up sheer mountain-sides, along narrow ridges, climbing over the buttress-like roots of tall trees and cutting through underbrush. We crossed swift-flowing mountain streams rushing with deceptively clear water, but the missionaries who knew about these things would not let us drink it. They said it was contaminated with the corpses of wild pigs and monkeys and was teeming with assorted germs. This particular trip, which almost finished me, was made by men of over fifty. To the un-Christian merriment of the rest of us, one of the reverend gentlemen fell into the river.

The inter-related problems of food and health were the greatest worry in the camp. Strangely enough, the children were completely healthy and vigorous, including two babies under one year of age. The week before I had arrived a boy was born, and the baby and his mother were perfectly healthy. The grown-ups were generally fairly healthy, but did not have a sufficient margin of strength, and this grew progressively smaller. Living for months in the jungle, where it was rarely completely dry, and almost never seeing the sun, they had become pale, and tropical ulcers had developed on their legs. None of the missionaries suffered from malaria while I was there. They all slept under nets, but in the darkness of the forest the anopheles mosquitoes bit severely in the daytime as well as at night. The natives in the surrounding hills suffered a lot from this scourge. The camp had few medicines of any sort.

Rice, corn and sweet potatoes were their staple foods. There were some vegetables and fruits, but the diet almost completely lacked meat or fish. A few had chickens, but these did not do well, as they found little food to scratch in the dark forest. What few eggs they laid went to those who were weakest and to nursing mothers. There were never any food reserves, and often rations had to be cut. The diet kept them alive, but only just, considering the heavy work they had to do and during the time I was there they grew noticeably weaker.

When things looked particularly grim the missionaries would say special prayers and they were usually answered. Natives would come with gifts of vegetables or fruit, or some new Chinese trader on the coast would make them a loan. They were always short of cash, and the Chinese traders progressively cut their credit.

The feats of organization and courage which had produced this camp were amazing, but not unique. In other parts of these islands, and elsewhere in the Pacific, similar stories of organized hideouts could be told. What set "Forest Glen" apart was its spirit. The missionaries external circumstances were desperate and they must have known it in their hearts.

The Japanese had their nearest garrison at Zamboanga City, some sixty miles to the south-east, and it was probable that they already knew about the existence of the camp, although they may have been in doubt about its exact location. But even if they were unaware of it while I was in the area, only a miracle could prevent them from hearing about it in time.

So the missionaries waited. Because of their families and of the age of many of them, they had to stay where they were. They could not retreat farther into the jungle, and the sea was no help to them. They simply had faith in their God, whom they had served all their lives.

While they waited, they laughed and had fun. They had charades and games on Sundays, and no birthday passed without a party. They told me of the Fourth of July celebration and of the precious rations they were saving for the Christmas cake. Their gaiety was never forced or artificial, and they were quite unselfconscious.

In Manila and Iloilo I had seen people behave quite

differently in the face of the approaching enemy; the men of my type, the businessmen, bankers, engineers planters and public servants. In many cases they had been afraid, irresolute or had put on a false front of unconcern, and almost all of them had drifted. Compared to them, these missionaries, these poor relations of the white communities in the Far East, were heroes—that was the only word to describe them—but I don't think they ever thought of themselves as such.

What troubles and inner anxieties they had, they took to their Church and their prayer meetings. This attitude was not what was later known by the sardonic but apt name of "fox-hole religion". The people of "Forest Glen" had prayed all their lives.

On Sundays the community hall became a church. We all dressed in our best, such as it was. The eight ordained members of the camp preached in turn, and they had much to say that was comforting and sensible. In the afternoons short services were held for the natives in their surrounding little camps. At the same time, the energetic Miss Bohleen held a Sunday school for native and white children, away up on the knoll named after her.

On Sunday evenings, the Reverend Davis conducted a Bible-study class. When I arrived they had finished studying the Gospel of Luke and had started on the Psalms. I should have liked to do more reading, but it was impossible to light the place properly; kerosene and palm oil had to be rationed.

It was quite natural for me to be affected by the atmosphere. There were many discussions, and I liked best to talk to the Reverend Davis, a saintly old man with a mane of white hair. The natives in the surrounding hills adored him and built for him the best house. Before I left the camp, he presented me with a beautifully bound Bible, a wonderful and greatly treasured gift.

Perhaps my favourite was the Reverend Christie. He was

a small man, about my age whose legs had been almost useless since childhood, so that he had to be carried everywhere. He had that gentle and serene disposition which is sometimes given to those who are seriously ill or crippled, as if to compensate them for what their bodies lack. He was completely without guile and had a lovely smile.

My seven weeks with these good Christian people was an experience I shall never forget.

All of a sudden it was October again, time to think of returning to Labason and to "Maring". There was no war news, only rumours, which was worse than no news at all. There were reports of sporadic guerilla activities in the peninsula, and several Filipinos in Japanese pay were said to have been shot. There was nothing in the news to influence my plan, but the missionaries were anxious that I should change my route. Some of them had come from Jolo, where they had lived and worked for twenty years, and they warned me of the Moros' bloodlust, their treachery and piracy. They told me stories of "running amok", that malady of the sun which made a man run through the streets with the strength of three, killing with a kris for no reason, until he himself was brought down by the shots of a policeman. His arms, legs, thighs and chest were first tightly bound with thin strips of cloth, so that he would not be weakened too quickly by the loss of blood from any one shot. It took a bull's eye with a ·45 bullet to stop him, and the Constabulary still used that calibre in the Sulu province, after having changed over to ·32 calibre everywhere else in the islands. I was shown a gory photograph of a decapitated body, the victim of amok, in which the head had rolled several yards away from the force of the blow.

Apparently running amok also had some religious significance, for the more people the amok-runner killed before coming to his inevitable end, the better it would be for the Moslem in the next world. To slay an unbeliever, and especially a Christian, was a particularly Good Thing, assuring the Moro not only of a corner seat in one of the better-class heavens of the Koran but a trip there on a snow-white horse.

I wrote down the Moro stories as they were told to me, and I respected the missionaries' warnings. I had heard the same stories everywhere in the islands, and I knew from my own experience that I would be taking my life in my hands in Moro country, but I felt that that was a risk I had to take. There were other risks, even greater, and I must stick to my carefully thought-out plan.

My trader friend still did not report, and the missionaries made arrangements to have me taken back to Labason with one of their connections. I was definitely going to leave them around 10th October.

Two days before the date fixed for my departure the camp had a farewell meeting in my honour. There were games and speeches, and I was presented with envelopes containing slips with scripture quotations made by all camp members. One was to be read each day on my trip. The envelope was decorated by Mrs. Davis with a ship and inscribed with Verses 23 and 24 of Psalm 107. This was one of the few Psalms I knew by heart, and I had often thought how appropriate these verses were:

> "They that go down to the sea in ships, that do business in great waters;
> "These see the works of the Lord, and his wonders in the deep."

I always like that. It was not only true, but also it was very beautiful English.

The next day the camp was under a cloud. Word had come from the natives that the Japanese would get there in a month or two. It was one of those rumours that one did not know whether to believe or not. The people of "Forest

Glen" put it from them and went about their business. There was nothing else for them to do.

The weather was now improving, and the following day a fine north wind blew and Alvarez at last turned up. He sent a message that he was anchored by the shore in his vinta "Mabuhai", which was Tagalog for Good Luck.

Saying goodbye to the camp was not easy, but my continued presence could do no good. On the contrary, I was the only one who was not in some way connected with missionary work, and if the Japanese were to find me there it might compromise the whole community.

The day was a Sunday, and they were all gathered in their best dresses shortly before the morning service. The children were down from Sunday school and they would not let me go. There had been many partings for me in these islands during the last nine months, but this was the hardest of all.

Three of the younger men came to the shore with me down the valley track up which I had first climbed seven weeks earlier. They helped me to carry my possessions and enough food for the journey.

"KAKUGAN"

There was no doubt we were at sea again. The first night a duster drove our vinta shorewards, and although Alvarez did a beautiful job of sail-handling, we were drenched in the surf and our belongings likewise. That night I slept in wet clothes for the first time in many weeks.

I was getting to know the Zamboanga coast by now, and the more I saw of it, the better I liked it. There was an endless variety of scenery, and Alvarez knew every nook and cranny. The following day we anchored inside one of the typical smaller Mindanao streams; we entered over a bar a little way out at sea, then through a narrow opening in the shore line and found ourselves in a sort of lagoon, more or less filled with nipah swamps and mangroves. The nipah is not a beautiful palm, but a very useful one with its long scraggy fronds, which seem to grow straight out of the swamp. After the leaves are cut they are thoroughly dried, and nothing more is necessary to make of them the long-lasting waterproof building material for roofing and wall-covering that is seen throughout the islands.

From passing vintas we heard about clashes between the Japanese and our guerillas at Labason, and now I could not get back quickly enough. But the winds were from the north. We had a crew aboard and did quite a bit of paddling, but it was slow work.

Near Sibuko Bay we heard that the Japanese and their Filipino policemen were patrolling the area both ashore and at sea, and thought it wise to lie low. My anxiety about "Maring" after the alarming news from Labason made any delay hard to take, but it would have been foolhardy to risk meeting a Japanese patrol at this stage, and we anchored in a small inlet for the day.

We sailed shortly after sunset, and throughout one of the most perfect nights I had experienced on this coast. The night breeze from the mountains was cool and smelled of the forest, the graceful vinta slid through the smooth water with only a gentle lap-lap along outriggers and hull, while the Zamboangenio crew sang in their soft, melodious voices. These were things to be remembered: the singing in the warm and clear night, drinking the water of young coconuts on a hot day, and the camp-fire dinners of rice and fish eaten off green leaves.

We reached Labason after three days. When our vinta passed over the bar early in the morning somehow the atmosphere was wrong. There was no one about, the town was deserted. My first thoughts were for "Maring". But there she was, securely moored in the river and looking quite happy. That was a great relief.

Chia and Friend were in town, and from them I heard a

125

most extraordinary story. No, it had not been the Japanese who had made the trouble, their invasion of the Philippines was an irritating side-show compared to the everlasting battle between the Moros and the local Filipino settlers. Again Labason had been the arena, and a regular pitched battle had been fought there the previous week. This must have been the uproar which we had heard about and which caused us such anxiety.

Labason had become a ghost town, and the only people who lurked in the streets were the Volunteer Guards, our guerillas. They had a dual task now, at least in theory. They had to fight the Moros as well as the Japanese.

Gradually I pieced the story together from the accounts of Friend, Chia and others.

Of all places, the raiding party of Moros had come from the Sangboys, and the Panglima Sabdani appeared to have been the chief culprit. This made my position extremely delicate, because I had friends in both camps, and particularly as the first thing Sabdani had said when he saw Friend was, "Where is my son?"

It appeared that about twenty-five large Moro cumpit boats had gathered at Murcielagos Island opposite Labason, preparatory to a full-fledged invasion—a cumpit is a larger vinta and carries the same type of sail, but instead of out-riggers, these boats have round bilges.

One boat, with Sabdani and seven men aboard, had come over to Labason, where they anchored along the river-bank. Sabdani and three men had then walked to the centre of the town, leaving four men with the ship. The Panglima was in full war regalia, complete with kris and an armband with the Japanese flag, which he must have acquired from Zamboanga since I left. He had behaved offensively and asked in the bazaar to be shown to the "Office". He was then required to let himself be disarmed, while covered by a number of shotguns.

Meanwhile, the armed villagers had dispatched an inspection party to his cumpit, the crew of which started the trouble by firing shotguns at the oncomers. None of the villagers was hurt, the fire was returned and two Moros were killed.

Then a villager was despatched to report to the group holding palaver near the bazaar, and arrived running and shouting, "Shoot them, shoot them". At this, guns went off and three of Sabdani's companions dropped dead, but the Panglima, a wily old gentleman who had done this sort of thing before, had wisely situated himself so that shots in his direction would endanger innocent bystanders, among whom was Friend. Then he did some pretty nippy work ducking in and out of passages to get back to his boat. He was fired upon several times in vain, but he managed to cut down and kill an old man with a scythe he grabbed from him, and the cumpit made good her escape. The corpses of the two Moros killed in the boat would probably be taken to the Japanese at Zamboanga as exhibit "A".

I would have given much to see the old rogue in action, but I was shocked about the news of his wearing an armband with a Japanese flag, which was the sign of submission to their authority. I could not believe that the Panglima had gone over to the Japanese side; it was completely out of character after he had condemned them so vigorously when I was at Sangboy in July. I decided that he was a shrewd fox and paid the Japanese lip service to retain his official position on Sangboy and to use them in support of his unceasing campaign against the Filipinos on Mindanao.

My position now seemed to me precarious. I did not fear so much a fresh Moro assault as a punitive expedition from the Japanese. There was nothing for me to do but to hurry forward the fitting out of "Maring". The possibility of being caught by the Japanese gave me enough to worry about without getting myself mixed up in local wars.

Chia was as good as his word. The new sail, of grey

sheeting, was being made and although the material was not ideal, it was a wonder that it was available at all.

Chia made me a most welcome present, a tin of "Capstan" pipe tobacco, my favourite brand and a rare luxury. For months past I had been experimenting with native tobacco. This was particularly strong and suitable only for very dark cigars, which I did not enjoy. Converting this stuff for pipe use was quite a trick if I was not to go green every time I took a puff, and everybody had a different recipe. The one I adopted in the end required the leaves to be washed three or four times, then dried and cured with molasses, and I laid in a good supply of this.

When I returned to my lodgings in Friend's house I made an unhappy discovery. All the personal belongings I had brought from Manila had been stolen out of my kit-bag. The thief was some traveller who had slept in my room, and he had substituted the missing bulk in the bag by filling it with coconut husks. I was now reduced to a few khaki shirts and shorts, but did not feel too upset; I had lost much more than that to thieving Filipinos. Fortunately, Friend had kept my compass and charts in his own bedroom, and they were quite safe. They were all that really mattered.

The south-west monsoon was now at an end. The weather cleared and the wind shifted into the north. I now had a feeling of urgency and I began working on "Maring" to fit her for single-handed sailing again. Nothing much appeared to be wrong except that her deck needed caulking. The water drum and jars also had to be carefully placed in position again, and I was determined that everything would be ready to leave on Saturday 24th October. Meantime I tried to secure rice and sugar for the missionary camp. Both Friend and Chia promised their help.

21st October, the third day before I was due to sail, was altogether a very irregular day. It started badly in the morning when I discovered a serious leak in "Maring's" forepeak.

The previous day I had bailed considerable quantities of what I thought was rain-water, but that morning I was surprised to find her full again. This would be a complicated repair.

Next, around eight o'clock when I returned to breakfast we had a heavy earthquake. It lasted for more than a minute, and the shocks were so severe that one could scarcely stand up without help. Then shortly afterwards, a tidal wave tore "Maring" from her moorings and sent her upstream. Luckily she was deposited undamaged on a sandbank, and the natives said afterwards that "Maring" had evacuated herself.

The next unlooked-for event was the most momentous of all. Later in the morning Lieutenant Melicor introduced a young Filipino Army officer to me. Second Lieutenant Frank Young. He was twenty-two years old, a Mestizo with an American father and a Moro mother, and when the Japanese came into the War he had been stationed in the north of Luzon and had been in the thick of the fighting there. He was not in uniform, and I asked to see his credentials, which he produced readily.

Lieutenant Young had a startling proposition to make. For reasons of his own he wanted to go to Australia, and he asked me to come along with him. He had heard of "Maring" and of me, and was very anxious that I should be one of his party. He himself had no knowledge of navigation, and would otherwise have to rely on the somewhat haphazard methods of Moro pilots, whom he intended to pick up in the Tawi-Tawi group farther south. Also, we were to take his wife and small child to her home island south of Jolo. Young himself had been born somewhere around there.

This was an unexpected development, and I could not bring myself even to consider the idea of leaving "Maring". I took Young over to her, but he was not impressed. He considered my boat much too small and unsuitable for southern waters, where a vinta or cumpit rig would be less conspicuous than "Maring's" fore-and-aft sail plan. He also said that we could not take a crew along in my boat and that he would definitely not entrust himself to me but intended travelling with Moros. When I asked him what type of boat he had in mind, he said he proposed to use Army authority to requisition a large cumpit locally for which he would drum up a Moro crew.

It was a startling suggestion, and I asked him to wait for a day or two while I thought his scheme over and discussed it with Friend and Chia.

My friends and I debated half through that night. There were a number of advantages as well as dangers in both schemes. But from the first, I decided that I would not go with Young except on the clear understanding that I would be left in sole and complete charge of the vessel and of her navigation.

I tried to work out the pros and cons by myself. Sailing alone in "Maring" would solve the crew problem. After all I had seen and heard, I was reluctant to have anything to do with Moros—or half Moros—on a small-boat trip which would tax everyone to the limit, and would place me at their mercy. Also, provisioning and rationing for four or more people would be very much more of a problem than providing for one.

On the other hand, there would be a number of advantages in going with Lieutenant Young. The argument that "Maring's" rig would be strange in southern latitudes was a powerful one. Moro rigs and similar sail arrangements were a common sight all the way down to Timor, and this would heighten the chances of inspecting Japanese vessels taking us for harmless native traders or fishermen. Sailing with a larger crew would also ease the strain on my own endurance. I could probably teach them quickly how to steer a compass course, and while we were in Philippine waters I need not bother much about navigation, anyway.

Thus I could hope to sail the boat round the clock, make a faster trip and at the same time get more sleep than I would in "Maring". More sleep was a powerful inducement.

Friend said that it was my duty to get Lieutenant Young through to Australia, and there was some justice in that argument. Thus the pros and cons were almost balanced, but not quite. I had met Young less than twenty-four hours before and did not know him. His firm refusal to come alone with me in "Maring" had not been impressive. He was probably as wary of me as I was of him.

My first impression of the man had been neutral. He was rather tall and held himself well. He was thin and angular in his movements. His face was not unsympathetic, but it could not be called an open face; the mouth was thin lipped and wide, the nose sharp and short. He had very high cheek-bones and eyes of light colour and deeply sunk. The expression was all Moro, that same intense stare which bored through you but did not reveal very much. But his smile was quick and ready, and his manner was pleasant. I did not know what to make of him.

How could I risk it alone with a man I did not know? On ocean trips in small boats, even brothers and close friends are inclined to get on each other's nerves and to quarrel violently. I had read a lot about that, and it stood to reason.

I thought that if he was so keen to go to Australia he should come in my boat, but that he had refused to do. I was undecided, but strongly favoured continuing alone in "Maring"—the devil I knew.

The decision came the next day, and it had never really been mine to make. Young and Melicor took it for granted that I would fall in with their plan and would not hear of any objection. Both men were commissioned officers in the Army of their country, which gave them a status which I lacked, and although Lieutenant Melicor never hinted that he could use force if he wished, the possibility was not lost on any of us.

After I had sought and received a fresh assurance from Young that I would be left in complete charge of navigating the new boat, I decided to team up with him and to abandon the trip in "Maring".

From that moment events moved fast. Young was in a hurry, and intended us to sail the following day, 24th October, and once I had made the decision I threw myself into the preparations unreservedly. Further hesitation would be folly. Every day counted, now that the north wind had begun to blow.

The first thing I did was to sell "Maring" to Friend, for one hundred and seventy-five pesos. I hoped she would serve him as well as she had served me. The water drum and other stores were taken out of her, and with the money from the sale more provisions were bought.

Lieutenant Young and I "requisitioned" a cumpit called "Kakugan", which was Moro for Good Fortune. Helped by the local guerillas, we simply took her from one of the less-popular Chinese traders. To make the requisition legal, we valued the boat fairly, at three hundred pesos. The wealthy Chinaman was issued with a receipt for this amount signed by Young and myself, witnessed by Lieutenant Melicor and Friend. He struggled and gasped a bit, and even tried to hide "Kakugan's" rudder, but had to give in after being "persuaded" by Lieutenant Melicor. I could not understand what they said, but was told that threats of violence and of delivery to the Japanese were among the arguments. The transaction would certainly not have been ethical under normal conditions, but conditions were abnormal, and I hadn't the slightest doubt that the Chinaman would soon get himself another boat and continue trading and getting the better of the simple hill tribes as before.

We hired a crew of three Moros, whose loyalties were said to be proven. Sahibad, the oldest of them, who would function as sailing master, was thirty and the only married man, apart from Young. The other two Moros, Sabdal and

Ali, were strong young fellows, relatives of Sahibad. All came from Sangboy. It was strange and somehow mysterious how all the roads led to and from that tiny island ever since I had come down to Mindanao.

With so much man-power, "Kakugan" was quickly fitted out. She was an open boat except for a small decked-in fo'c'sle and poop, and removable floorboards, placed half-way between keel and sheerstrake formed the deck for the rest of the boat. Provisions were stored on racks under the floorboards, and water was carried in two sixty-gallon drums, my old one from "Maring" and another one just like it, and in one twenty-gallon stone jar; all were placed aft, one behind the other. We would sleep on mats on the flat floor and the cooking would be done in a small well deck just forward of the poop. We carried the customary five-gallon tin stoves, and a plentiful supply of firewood was stored under the forepeak. Oars, awnings, personal belongings and odds and ends were shipped on top of and underneath two narrow shelves running on both sides of the main deck in a fore-and-aft direction, fitted about eighteen inches above the floorboards. We intended to carry the same types of provisions on which I had lived in "Maring" and, in addition, we bought dried fish from Chia. Cassava paste and coconuts were to be taken on farther south. "Maring's" purchase money went quickly, and before we sailed I was broke again.

Security arrangements were now made by Young and myself with the assistance of Friend and Lieutenant Melicor. My diary entry of 24th October on this subject reads:

> "Crisscross safety arrangements have been made, i.e. if one party tries to back out, or double-cross, the other chops his head off. Sounds ugly but is only reasonable. Crew's family held at Labason for hostage."

What it meant was that Sahibad's family was to be kept at Labason as hostages to the safety of Lieutenant Young and

133

of myself. They were to be kept under observation by Lieutenant Melicor and would not be allowed to leave the area controlled by his force without a special permit. The arrangement sounded quite fantastic to me, but the others accepted it as a matter of course. Life was cheap around Moro land at all times, and Young and I had to have some trump cards to play if the crew should feel like changing their minds.

At that moment the crew were most enthusiastic and willing to go wherever Young and I went. I repeatedly tried to point out to them the hazards of the voyage, the possible duration of it, the risks and the difficulties of returning. They said they appreciated all that, but were willing to take the risk. As I spoke no Moro, unfortunately all this had to be done through Frank Young as interpreter. He had much of their blood and outlook and had spent his childhood among them.

So far as I could discover, there was not one single clear-cut reason for their eagerness, but many contributing factors. They had formed a violent hatred of the Japanese, and the idea of taking an Army officer and a white man away from them had much appeal. Further, as a half-Moro and an officer in the Army, Frank Young's orders carried weight with them. They also had a liking for adventure for its own sake, and the trip sounded like a lot of fun. Finally—and this argument weighed strongly—wealth and glory were held out to them if we were successful. Wealth in this connection meant wrist-watches, pistols and clothing, promises which Young and I felt we could make them in good faith.

Before we sailed, Young and I discussed the command set-up. We agreed to be Joint-Masters and, in addition, I was to be Navigator. I agreed to explain my courses and route to him as we went along. In return—and on my repeated insistence—Young accepted the proposition that in any argument about the handling of the vessel, or of its navigation and routes, mine was to be the deciding voice. It was a curious arrangement, but understandable, considering that the two parties who made it had known each other for only three days.

Frank Young was sincere, helpful and very willing, but on his own admission he did not know the first thing about navigation. He had never seen a boat's compass before, and small-boat work was unknown to him except as a passenger on short trips from island to island. His notions of geography were hazy and his knowledge of seamanship was nil. From the first day to the last, the responsibility for the safety of the crew and for the entire venture remained mine alone.

The wind was blowing steadily out of the north. All my things were now aboard. I said goodbye to the friends I had made in Labason, to Chia, Lieutenant Melicor and to Horace Friend.

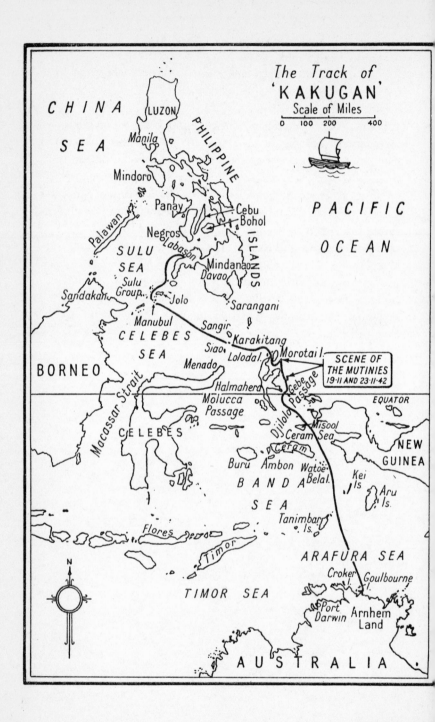

V. FORTY-SEVEN DAYS OUT

RETURN TO SANGBOY

"KAKUGAN" sailed at three in the afternoon on Saturday, 24th October 1942, with Frank Young, myself, three crew—Sahibad, Sabdal and Ali—and four passengers: Frank Young's wife and small daughter, another Filipino woman and Young's Army batman, who were to be dropped on an island farther south. A small group of well-wishers on the shore waved to us, and with a push and a shove we were off. The big square sail was set and a strong off-shore breeze took us out of the bay.

We did not get very far on that first day. The usual afternoon rain squalls hit us and drenched everything on board and, as usual at the outset of most sea voyages, whether short or long, in liners or in small boats, "Kakugan" was in chaos. After sailing three miles, we anchored in the lee of Murcielagos Island to spend the night and make things shipshape.

It was soon discovered that "Kakugan" leaked quite a bit and, moreover, all rain-water ran into her bilges because she was not decked-in. That meant more bailing from the well deck aft, her deepest point. A tin and a coconut shell were used for this purpose, "Kakugan" did not even have a pump. We lit our first fire on board and had a lavish evening meal, rice, fresh fish and some of the delicacies given to us by our friends at Labason. Although I offered to help, the crew would not let me share in the cooking, cleaning and stowing, except to supervise; the mere suggestion seemed to shock them. This was quite an agreeable change after the back-breaking round-the-clock work during the first thirty days' trip in "Maring".

The plan was the same that I had worked out for "Maring" three months earlier. We were to leave Philippine waters from one of the islands south of Jolo in the Sulu Archipelago striking south-eastwards across the Celebes Sea and the Molucca Passage, then proceed due south through the Ceram and Arafura Seas to the Australian coast at Arnhem Land.

Until we left the Philippines, I was content to let the crew set the pace and sail the ship, as they knew both the boat and these waters intimately, whereas I had a lot to learn and, on the first shake-down part of the trip, I knew I should have to spend much time working out my plans for navigation.

The system of navigation was to be Dead Reckoning, a method of tracing a ship's course by plotting on paper, courses steered and estimated distances made good. The first thing was to try and work out a system of recording courses and distances. For this purpose I made pencil enlargements to scale of the coastlines and islands near which we were to pass. These drawings I called worksheets, and details for them were taken from the Dutch map I had, and from the copies of Admiralty Index Charts which I had made in the camp of the missionaries.

To take bearings, I cut a triangular notch in the compass casing, atop the lubber line. Opposite this notch on the casing, I tacked a small nail. Thus I had a simple sight, as on a rifle, which I could level at the point of which bearings were to be taken.

Of the two factors involved in Dead Reckoning, namely course steered and distance run, I had provided for the reasonably accurate recording of the first by means of the compass. Distance run, that is to say, made good over ground, had to be estimated, because we had no log to measure the boat's progress. I had had a fair amount of practice in estimating speed from pre-war yachting.

To navigate with an acceptable degree of accuracy by Dead Reckoning it was necessary to plot on paper every change of course, and also to note every increase and decrease in the boat's speed. Throughout the day and night these alterations were noted. Once every twenty-four hours the day's aggregate result was plotted on the worksheets in the form of a pencilled cross representing the new noon position. I kept this up throughout the trip, and it did the trick, even though I made many errors.

The beauty of navigation by Dead Reckoning was that I could re-establish my exact position with each new land-fall, provided that this landfall was recognized and identified exactly on a map. There were many islands in the waters we crossed and I thus had frequent checks on the accuracy or otherwise of my calculations. Cumulative errors could creep in only between two recognized landfalls.

To plot bearings on paper, I made a protractor out of a piece of semi-transparent oil paper with the help of a pair of dividers. A straight piece of bamboo made a good ruler. My compass was graded in points, and all courses were reckoned and plotted accordingly. Working by degrees in a very small ship was impracticable anyway, and to steer a small boat accurately to within half a point was a satisfactory job.

The proper way of navigating a ship is by celestial naviga-tion. But this was out because I had neither tables, sextant nor chronometer. But even had I possessed these aids, I am not sure that it would have made much difference. I am pretty hopeless with most kinds of figures. For us, Dead Reckoning proved sufficient, not only because I worked hard at it every day but also because a sixth sense of finding the way over the waters came to my aid. I don't know whether or not this feeling for navigation can be acquired. It is com-pounded of many things. Often during the coming weeks, I would wake for no apparent reason at all, look at the com-pass and find that the helmsman was a point or two off course. The way the water sounded when the stem bit into the waves, the feel of the wind on my face, the look of clouds and stars, and the rise and fall in the burbling noise of the wake, all had a meaning and helped me to keep our direction.

For another day we remained weather-bound on Murcie-lagos with rain and foul winds. The time was well used to stow rice and other provisions, and I was able to take a good look at this boat which was to be my home and my command for many weeks.

"Kakugan" was about thirty-five feet long, with a beam of approximately nine feet. She had very fine lines and a good turn of speed. Her draft was shallow, a little over two feet. Her mast was stepped well forward and carried a large Moro sail, lashed to two spars. The sailcloth was made of ordinary khaki drill, reinforced by us with some lengths of blue denim cloth bought at Labason.

The rig, of course, was the most extraordinary thing to a European: a square sail of about 450 square feet, marled to two bamboo spars, hoisted slantwise to a stumpy mast, so that from afar it looked like a diamond. Two-fifths of the upper spar, gaff or yard, were forward of the mast, while the end of the lower spar, boom or lower yard, was lashed to a beam on the fo'c'sle. The heavy sail was hoisted by a one-part halliard running through a slit in the masthead, and it required three strong men to set it. Sheaves, blocks, bitts, belaying pins and cleats were unknown luxuries. All rigging and the halliards were made fast to a rail running the length of the ship above the bulwarks, and to a crossbeam over the poop. The one-part mainsheet, and the two braces, or guy lines, of the upper spar—with which three ropes the sail was worked—were likewise lashed to the same rails. This arrangement sounded and was indeed very primitive, but had one great advantage: ropes could at all times be made fast in exactly the correct position relative to the prevailing set of sail, strength of wind and swell running. The halliard also did double duty as main backstay, and three more stays were set up, to windward and aft. The only part of the running rigging exposed to any chafe was the halliard at the place where it passed through the slit in the mast top. I vainly tried to grease that part of the halliard with soap; at this waste the Moros first gasped and then laughed. The pressure was great, and Sahibad had to freshen the nip at least twice daily.

We carried six oars, which gave us a speed of around two knots in a calm. Ground tackle was quite simple and consisted of one crooked wooden plough anchor weighed with a stone, native fashion. This insufficient equipment worried me at times when I thought of the many shoal areas we would have to pass.

At last the weather cleared and we left with a stiff evening breeze almost dead astern. We fairly bowled along the Zamboanga peninsula in the gathering dark, course set towards my old home, the Sangboy Islands. It was great running, and the boat was very fast compared to "Maring". During that first night of full sailing I took the morning watch from 2 to 6 a.m., and for the first time I realized fully how much there was for me to do, how much to learn and how difficult the crew were likely to be.

We kept on course for Sangboy, and there was talk of exchanging our boat there for a faster one, belonging to Sahibad's relatives. I had not intended calling when we sailed, remembering Sabdani's Japanese armband and what had happened at Labason only two weeks earlier, but the crew informed us calmly that they were going to Sangboy anyway, and Sahibad assured us that the old man had not changed his mind about the Japanese, and that he only went to their garrison at Zamboanga to be confirmed as Chief of Sangboy to save his island from the appointment of an outright Quisling Chief. This sounded plausible enough and was in line with the actions of many Filipino officials throughout the Archipelago whose basic loyalties to their country and to the United States were unquestionable. Since a call on the island was not far out of our way, I did not feel like making an issue of it while still in Moro territory and more dependent on the crew's goodwill than we would be later on. Moreover, I had half promised the Panglima Sabdani to see him on my way down.

During these first days the crew did pretty much as they liked, and Frank and I took back seats. I was satisfied to leave it at that and to put on the reins of discipline gradually, hoping to have the ship in good order and in a happy mood by the time we left Philippine waters.

While we sailed along the familiar waters Frank Young told many stories about the hard and cruel fighting in northern Luzon. He was a likeable chap, very impulsive and determined to see the thing through.

Gradually we got to know each other. Frank and his wife played with their little baby daughter, whom they called "Babing" and other affectionate names in their soft language. We also had with us Chris, a Philippine Army private, who had attached himself to Young somewhere in the central islands as his batman. He was not a sailor, and the crew made him do all the dirty work. Apart from Young and myself, he was the only Christian on board, and the Moslem crew bullied him a lot before he was put on shore later on.

During this early part of the trip we made our weapons ready, such as they were. Firearms we had none, but everybody had a barong or a kris, and in addition, Frank had a small fearsome-looking dagger. For use as artillery, the boys made some hand grenades out of a few sticks of dynamite bought from Chia at Labason for the purpose. The crew were very experienced about this, and had obviously done it many times before. The dynamite, a smelly yellowish-brown paste which looked harmless enough, was formed into a cylindrical shape and wrapped into stiff oiled paper, the original wrapping material. Now a number of thick nails, bits of iron and even stones were wrapped into a parcel with the dynamite in the middle and secured with lengths of stout rattan fibre. This package was fitted loosely in an empty cylindrical sardine tin and chocked down with more nails and assorted hardware. The lid of the tin was then pressed down and tied with more rattan. Now a hole was made in the tin with a sharp nail right down to the dynamite. Into this hole a black fuse was to be inserted when the time came. A workman-like job, in which Sahibad took great pride.

Watching the ammunition factory at work I wrote in my diary: "I hope to God we may not need these 'eggs'."

This hope looked like being disappointed shortly afterwards when we met a Japanese patrol boat. It happened in brilliant sunshine with only a light breeze blowing which did not permit us to sail more than about three knots. As both the Japanese launch and our boat were on converging courses, it would have aroused suspicion if we had altered course too violently, and there was nothing for it but to keep on. I wrote in my diary a few minutes after it was all over:

"Ship made ready for a fight, Moros put on their charm belts, bits of Moslem amulets covered with cloth. Sahibad prayed Moslem prayers into a coconut which he threw overboard. The belief is that the powerful prayers will deflect the course of a pursuing ship. The programme was: first bluff, and should that fail, hand grenades, kris and barongs. All was ready and our crew had a determined appearance. Whatever else they may be, I do not think they are cowards! Much against my will and inclinations, I had to keep under cover in the beginning, for a white man would have made inspection a certainty. The beat of the engines came closer and we all thought we were in for it, but the launch passed forty yards astern and kept on her course, without hailing us! Maybe the coconut prayers did the trick but then, probably the crew of the launch wanted to reach Zamboanga by supper-time and decided not to bother with just another Moro cumpit. Our relief could easily be imagined! Great exhilaration and handshaking."

143

The next day we reached Sangboy Island; it was almost like coming home. My foster-father, the Panglima Sabdani, came on board, wearing his armband with the Japanese flag on it. I had an anxious moment, but need not have worried, he had not changed, and truly received me as a son. The first thing he did was to present me with a dagger. The blade was sharp and business-like, and sheath and grip were decorated with silver filigree.

"Kakugan" remained at Sangboy for five days while we worked to make her ready in every respect for the big trip. Our provisions had to be re-stowed several times before everything looked right, and we had to take on water and coconuts. There was also talk about re-shuffling the crew, most of whom came from Sangboy or from neighbouring islands.

As on my first visit to Sangboy in July, I led a busy social life.

I was amazed at the change which had come over the place in the three months since I had been there. Taking heart at the Japanese lack of interference, most of the evacuees had returned, and the tiny island had a prosperous and almost festive appearance. Many boat owners now engaged in the smuggling trade, which had boomed as soon as regular steamer sailings ceased. Vintas and cumpits sailed north in fleets, loading rice and sugar on Negros for the Sulu Islands, or for Sandakan in British North Borneo, to be exchanged against coffee, rope and such manufactured articles as were still available. The trade was illegal, and the Japanese attempted to control it at the bigger ports, but the sea was big, and most smugglers got through with good profits. "Mundos," the Moro pirates, occasionally nabbed the traders at sea, but that was a risk the fighting Moros were always willing to take.

I saw the Moros at their best on this second occasion when I spent much time visiting from house to house with my "father". Everywhere I was made welcome with friendliness, given food and coffee and treated like one of the family.

One evening, they had a sort of feast and prayer-meeting in our honour, a customary combination in Moslem lands. We sat in a large circle on finely woven mats while the Hadji prayed and chanted and the chorus repeated certain passages with gusto, their bodies swaying in time to the music. It was a sight not easily forgotten; the dark interior and the swarthy be-turbaned faces of the Moro braves dimly lit by coconut-oil lamps.

I felt curiously reminded of the scene in the Arab Sheik's tent in Galsworthy's "Flowering Wilderness", which I had re-read so recently at Iloilo, and could well imagine the fanaticism which forced Wilfrid Desert to recant his religion. Fortunately, no such demand was made on me.

After praying, a good meal was served from small porcelain dishes grouped on large ornamented brass trays. There were fish dishes, rice, curried chicken and coffee and a fine sort of pastry made of rice flour. One dish, a thick and heavy sort of rice paste, tasted similar to "Mochi", a sweet eaten in Japan during the New Year festivities.

At night, Moro life appeared most acceptable and picturesque. The filth, the flies, the dirt, the ragged houses, the mangy cats and the unceasing spitting and betel-nut chewing were mercifully hidden by the dark, and the dim flares of the oil-lamps lit up only the faces, the colourful clothes and turbans, the flash of an ornamented kris handle, and transformed the scene inside the smallest hut into something out of the "Arabian Nights".

On Sabdani's insistence, I slept at his house, and slept very well indeed with the whole clan in the one large room of which the house consisted. They gave me a large sort of sarong as a combination blanket and night-shirt which worked admirably. No mother could have been more solicitous for her child than the old man was for me. It was difficult to believe that the loving foster-father who tenderly slipped an extra pillow under my head at night was the same fiend who had bloodily cut down and killed a defenceless old man at Labason less than a month ago.

Frank and his family stayed at another house, and they were treated with the same generous hospitality. But in spite of all the kindness shown to us, we were impatient to sail. However, the days were showery and we were weather-bound. It was so wet that we could not dry the boat out, and I was anxious about some of the food. Then Frank discovered provisions missing, half a sack of rice, some sugar and other things. This constant thieving was one of the less-attractive features of life in the Philippines.

But my greatest worry at this stage was how to put my-self and my ideas over to the crew. Young was rightly afraid of offending them, and said that our necks would not be worth anything once we got on their wrong side. Nevertheless, they had agreed to be in on this adventure with us, and they had to accept my orders.

The mere idea of preparing for a long sea voyage without stops all along the road was foreign to them all, including Frank Young. I just could not make them understand what I was driving at, and they thought it downright funny and miserly when I tried to insist on economy in the use of matches, kerosene, coconuts and the like. They could not understand that I was thinking of what things would look like in a month's time. My exhortations met with insignifi-cant success at first, but I had to persevere. Young asserted frequently that "everything is O.K." and I hoped he was not just following the line of least resistance. My biggest worry was how Sahibad and the rest of the crew would act once we left the Sulu Archipelago, when they would have to rely on my navigation and directions.

But on Sangboy I kept these thoughts to myself, and meanwhile the feasting went on.

There was to be a wedding, and we were invited. Sabdani had me dress in Moro clothes, purple trousers, a green shirt, white silk jacket with silver buttons and a multi-coloured turban to give the finishing touch. As side-arm I wore a beautiful long kris and looked what I was to the islanders, the adopted son of a Panglima. I did not, however, feel the part, but I was grateful to the old man for all the trouble he took. He showed me off like a proud father his first-born, and was completely serious and sincere about it. On the way to the wedding we went visiting from house to house, with coffee offered to us everywhere. The Moslem's religious veto on alcohol was a blessing. I shuddered to think how these hot-tempered people would behave when drunk. They were quick enough to kill and run amok as it was!

The Moros' love of colour was startling, but somehow their colour schemes never jarred and they always looked well dressed. At the wedding, the bride and 'groom had their faces painted with a spot design and looked very odd. The ceremony took place late in the afternoon and was short; there was some chanting by the Hadji, some shouting, and everything was over. She was the man's second wife, so the 'groom had been through it all before.

The Panglima told me that a Moro could have as many wives as he could conveniently support, and the story was told of a Datu from Jolo who had sixteen. Applying this economic yard-stick, I wondered whether it was possible to have half a wife only, but never found out.

We paid a call on our old friend the Hadji, who wore his green turban, signifying that he had made the sacred pilgrimage to Mecca. He lived in a nipah house by the mosque, which was a half-open pavilion made of rough boards. They were not too fussy about the sanctity of the place because "Kakugan's" sail was laid out there to be strengthened with new bolt ropes and cloth patches. The Hadji, a huge elderly man with a rough and rather stern face, was apparently pleased to see me, for he dished up the inevitable coffee and pastry. That I was an unbeliever was

147

apparently balanced in his estimate by my liking for the sea
and for sailing, which I shared with the islanders. He
rummaged in an old soap box and proudly produced a
cancelled third-class steamer ticket to Singapore and thence
to Arabia. This, together with some other English-written
documents, was the secular evidence of his holy mission. I
wished we could have done better in our conversation than
the curious mixture of gestures, Spanish, English, Moro and
Tagalog to which we were always reduced.

During the last days of October the weather cleared and
"Kakugan" was slowly made ready for sea. Negotiations
went on about the size and composition of our crew. The
Moros insisted that we must have more men "for all even-
tualities" and "to row the boat when there is no wind". I
was aware that these were mainly excuses, and that the real
reason behind this desire to increase the crew was a belief in
the saying that there is safety in numbers. Actually, "Kakugan" could have been handled comfortably by three men,
but I had little authority in the matter while we were ashore
on their island.

There was more trouble on my birthday, 30th October.
The year before, K. G. Stevens and I had celebrated it with
drinks at the Manila Hotel and a good dinner to follow.
This time there was another dinner-party of a different sort,
another wedding feast. I had hoped to sail the previous day,
but the crew would not hear of missing it and invented one
excuse after another.

While we were sitting packed like sardines in the nipah
house where the wedding took place, word went around
that a vinta with Moro policemen in Japanese pay had
arrived from the Japanese post at Isabella on Basilan Island,
south of Zamboanga. By the same mysterious telegraph
which we had seen function so often, our presence had
become known to the enemy, and they had come with the
intention of taking Young and myself to Isabella for
"inspection". Immediately the news became known,

Sahibad and his gang grabbed their side-arms, and those of the crew who were without theirs rushed to fetch them.

A few minutes later, while we were sitting and eating in the dark and crowded room, three swarthy Moros with shotguns entered. The atmosphere became tense and electric, all activity and talk stopped. The Panglima and the elders among whom Young and I were sitting, quietly formed a protective ring around us. Most of the younger men had their hands on the grip of their barongs, and the faces of our crew were a reassuring study in fighting spirit and determination. The three policemen, who had no insignia except their guns to proclaim their office, realized quickly that feeling was against them and that they would not stand a chance in the crowded room if they should try and use force. They sat down very politely at the other end of the room. Sabdani, as local Chief, whipped out his Japanese armband and went over to palaver with them. After it had been made quite clear to them that they could not carry out their arrests, the policemen took part in the eating and drinking and left shortly afterwards.

This incident was yet another sign that the sands were running out. The enemy's messengers would have four hours' sail back to Basilan, and we reckoned that this would give us the rest of the night and the early morning to finish our preparations and sail.

Everyone now became very anxious about our safety. I rested for a few hours in Sabdani's house, but nobody got much sleep. He and his two wives and the children kept me company, praying and helping us to get our belongings together. The Panglima laboured hard with pencil and paper and produced in Arabic script a number of identical slips of paper, each carrying a powerful Moslem prayer to foil the enemy. He exhorted me carefully, making use of Frank Young as interpreter, to keep the paper slips on my body and to use them only in great emergency, throwing one overboard astern when pursued by a hostile ship.

Before we left early the next morning we saw a touching sight: in front of the house where one of the weddings had taken place, the Moros had hoisted an American flag on a pole in honour of our leaving. After fighting against it for decades, the Moros and other citizens of the Philippines probably realized more than they had ever done before that it stood for something they had temporarily lost, just and fair government.

Then it was time to say goodbye. The Panglima Sabdani and I embraced, and there were tears in his eyes. I left good friends on Sangboy, and the Panglima Sabdani was the best of them all.

From now on it would be by God, by guess and by luck until we reached Australia.

LEAVING THE PHILIPPINES

In addition to Frank Young and myself, "Kakugan" had acquired a crew of six. There was Sahibad, chief of the crew and the oldest, to whom I had given the title of Sailing Master, and the sailors' names were Sabdal, Ali, Ajijohn, Dalil and Manguna.

We did not get far on the first day. A strong south-west wind blew up dead in our path, and we sheltered between a couple of small islands no bigger than football fields, each with a dazzling white beach, a few coconut palms and some smaller trees. There are thousands of these delightful uninhabited tiny islands in the Philippines, and many of them are found only on the most detailed naval charts.

We took aboard more firewood and coconuts and discovered a turtle's nest with over a hundred eggs buried in the sand and looking like a heap of new golf balls. It was a valuable find, although they tasted rather too strong for my liking.

The wind veered to the north, we raised the anchor and made our way to the south-west with the intention of

150

keeping well clear of the island of Jolo. As usual, we were taking an indirect route because of pirates and likely Japanese patrols along the direct trade route. Our course was for some small island south of Jolo, possibly Manubul, near Siasi, where we would drop our passengers.

The crew now became my main concern. They were incredibly slow and it was impossible to drive them. Young, in constant fear lest we should "offend" and literally lose our heads, was not much of a help. In my eight years in the East I had had to do at one time or another with all shades of Japanese, Koreans, Chinese, Tagalogs, and on the whole did not find it very difficult to discover my brothers under the skin. But these Moros were a law unto themselves, and my attempts to enforce discipline and order met with little understanding. Perhaps it was that they did not want to accept orders from a non-Moslem.

The worst trouble was usually about food. The boys felt offended whenever I tried to suggest economy. Regular meal-times were unknown, they stuffed themselves whenever they felt like it, and attempts to cut down on the daily ration provoked stubborn resistance. When I suggested that they should eat one dried fish with their rice instead of two or three, or that they should refrain from having a snack of young coconut just before meal-time, they glowered at me and murmured things obviously unpleasant and disrespectful, which Frank refused to translate for me. My argument that it was preferable to have one fish a day for two months instead of four fish a day for three weeks did not sink in, and the point of my setting an example by eating sparingly was lost completely. They probably thought I did not need more. What infuriated me more than anything was when they opened coconuts to drink the water only, throwing the nut with all the good meat overboard.

At the rate of consumption during those first days our provisions and water would not have lasted a month. I hoped to top up at least with water before attempting to cross the open Celebes Sea, then I would enforce economy somehow.

How well I understood the feelings of old-time sailing ship Mates, "hard cases", trying to keep a bunch of "furriners" in hand, and more than ever did I then realize what foul crimes mutiny and insubordination are at sea. The crew could not see that my actions were for their own good, that I was thinking of their welfare as much as my own.

What made the situation so difficult were mainly two factors, the primitive character of these boys and the danger of the whole undertaking. These illiterate Moros meant well, they longed for adventure and they were full of an impulsive sort of courage, but they had to be led if the expedition was not to end in capture by the Japanese.

Frank understood but was too weak and too deeply involved in Moro ways and traditions to exert the necessary pressure, but he did his best to support me in these early days. I hoped to form a bond of understanding with Frank, and with Sahibad when he realized the aim of my insistence —Sahibad was a seafaring man and had made the two-hundred-mile trip to Sandakan. But as for the crew, the need for hurry and constant exertion was lost on them. I could not even make them understand the need for cleaning the boat at least once a day. All manner of food scraps, fish bones and bits of rice led an undisturbed existence right on the poop.

I tried not to crack the whip too much, and on the whole things went quite well these first days, but I was increasingly worried about the likelihood of real friction when the need for stricter measures became imperative, especially in the open sea. I often prayed for Grace, for guidance and for my sense of humour not to desert me. Invariably my prayers were answered and regular reading of the Bible for a few minutes each day was a source of strength to me. I read systematically from the Old and New Testaments, and often from the Psalms. The Bible, which the Reverend Davis had given me as a farewell gift when I left "Forest Glen", and the "Philippine Pilot" were the only books aboard "Kakugan".

The weather now became quite pleasant and at midnight on 3rd November we rounded the western extremity of Jolo. We kept a respectful distance as we knew that this corner was frequented both by Japanese patrols and by Moro pirates looking for vessels coming down to the Tawi-Tawi and Sibuto groups with sugar and rice.

From the way the crew were talking it seemed that piracy was really the business to be in. The Japanese were newcomers to this game of cops and robbers and had other more pressing worries.

The "mundos" were said to have taken large numbers of firearms, including machine-guns, from disbanded Philippine Army units. It was as well we never met with them.

I worked on my navigation for at least an hour a day and began to feel more confident. One of the obstacles to accuracy was my ignorance of ocean currents, which were obviously strong and of varying directions in these confined waters. I explained the compass to Young and to Sahibad, for the three of us were to take alternate watches once we left Philippine waters. Young had a hazy idea of the thing from his infantry training, but the lubber line and floating card had him foxed for a while.

To Sahibad, and to the rest of the boys, the compass was a book with seven seals, which rather surprised me, seeing that their islands were not far away from China, the cradle of the compass. The Moro blue-water seamanship had become less of a universal accomplishment among them during the last half-century, and now only a few tribes, notably the men from the Tawi-Tawi and from the Ubian Islands, sailed as far south as Celebes, Borneo and Timor. Sahibad maintained that his people never sailed beyond Sandakan now, and that they hardly ever went out of sight of land.

To boost morale we talked of what we should do when

we reached Australia, as if that was a certainty. I promised my compass to Sahibad on our arrival, and a deck of playing-cards with which I had whiled away some weary days on Panay playing solitaire were to go to Sabdal. It looked far from a certainty whether I should ever be able to keep these promises; if I had been a marine underwriter I should have classed "Kakugan" as a poor risk just then.

The scenery of the Sulu Islands was a never-ending delight. What fun this voyage would have been in peace-time. We were becalmed during heavy rain off the north-west coast of Lapac Island, and when it stopped the islands stood out fresh and sparkling in the clear afternoon sun. Even the dry and matter-of-fact "Philippine Pilot" had a word of praise for this happy corner of the island world.

In the evening of 4th November we anchored on a reef south of Lapac and for the first time I saw Moro villages built over the water on stilts. I could not take more than an occasional peep over the bulwark, having to stay under cover because of police employed by the Japanese. After rounding Lapac west point in clearing weather, we were treated to a sight to make the heart of any lover of sailing-boats beat faster: on a smooth blue sea against a background of green islands, sailed great fleets of Moro boats—we had struck the trading route leading southward from Siasi to Tawi-Tawi.

There must have been at least a hundred of them, vintas and cumpits. The boats were of all sizes, and their sails blazed with colour in the hot afternoon sun. Some had triangular and striped patterns in their canvas, distinguish-ing and trade-marks, I was told. The rectangular sails, hoisted at an angle of forty-five degrees, looked like huge diamonds over the slender hulls, and billowed out with that perfection of shape which the wind gives to a well-cut sail. They looked fast, perky and daring, these Moro ships.

The sight was also reassuring to us. "Kakugan" had

joined the flock, we were just one boat among many, and felt very safe that day.

In the late afternoon we anchored at Manubul, to the south of Siasi, where we were to disembark our passengers, refresh ourselves with fruit and take on more food and water.

By the usual yet still mysterious means, our arrival at Manubul had been known for a week, the story being embellished as usual. We were said to have a machine-gun on board!

The family of Young's wife lived near by and soon appeared, and the rejoicing was great at seeing their daughter and her baby safe at last, after four months' of adventurous travel from Manila, which had included a full-fledged shipwreck off the coast of Leyte. In the evening the Young family and our other lady passenger disembarked, but I refused their kind invitation to spend the night ashore. I preferred not to tempt prowlers by leaving everything wide open. At this point, the theft of a sack of rice could mean the difference between the success and failure of our adventure.

As soon as we arrived, Sahibad and the crew went ashore to buy the remainder of our needs, including rope, fruit, another water jar and some more kajang rolls of nipah leaves interlaced with rattan. These made excellent but fragile awnings. The crew made a holiday of it, wearing their most flamboyantly-coloured trousers, blouses and sashes. Their only sorrow was that they had to leave their barongs on board. This was a prudent rule made long ago by the American administration and was apparently still enforced. Moro gentlemen were not allowed to go about armed in strange ports.

While anchored off Manubul I had a significant brush with the crew about wasting food. In the morning they had made a huge mess of fried rice and sugar. They ate a little, then had a meal ashore. When they came back at five in the afternoon they started to cook more rice, although the pan was still full with the morning's rice and sugar. When I forbade them to cook, and ordered that they eat what was left, they growled and refused to obey. Thereupon I made a fire, warmed up the morning rice and ate some myself to set an example. This left them unmoved, and they spoke up, saying the morning's rice would not be healthy now and they would rather not eat at all. I made this a test case and upheld my veto and there was bad feeling for a while, but I had to begin asserting authority.

The incident ended happily. Sabdal, one of our sailors, had a great sense of the comic, and after everybody had sulked for a while, he began to eat the warmed-up mess, pretending to be horribly sick afterwards. He rolled around the boat and gave a regular performance until the rest of the crew caught up with the spirit of things and everybody laughed. When the boys were in a good mood they were companionable and clownish.

We were all in excellent health, although tropical ulcers had begun to bother me again. My last pair of shoes had given out some little time before. On Sangboy I had walked barefoot, and some of the scratches collected there had begun to fester and ulcerate.

It took four days to get away from here, while the crew procrastinated and made the most of our last stay in Philippine territory. At last my patience came to an end and on 7th November I announced that we would sail that night— we had already wasted a morning of fair wind and tide, because drinking-water had not been brought aboard. We took on more provisions, bags of cassava paste, another sack of rice, bananas and mangoes, but unfortunately, no dried fish were procurable here. Another lack which worried me was kerosene; all we had were the two bottles I had started with in "Maring", which had been filled up again at Labason. We had to sail night and day, especially in the open sea, and depended on our kerosene-fed hurricane lamp to light the compass card.

156

I was in very low spirits all that day. My responsibility weighed heavily, there were so many weak points, so many unknown factors. My "navigation"—if it could be called such—was the weakest of all, and before us lay the first stage across blue water, at least four days out of sight of land, crossing the Celebes Sea. I was like the diver on the spring-board, and—like him—felt better the moment we were off.

CROSSING BLUE WATER

At 1 a.m. on Sunday, 8th November, we sailed away from the Philippines to a fair north-westerly breeze, and immediately ran into the dangerous narrow passage in the reef south of Siasi. "Kakugan" pitched heavily in the rapid-flowing current, and we had some anxious moments when several water-jars almost came adrift—if we had been broached our trip would have come to an early end. But we came through safely. I had had no idea of the strength of the current, or I should not have dared to risk the run at night while the tide was ebbing. After this experience, I could well believe the many stories still told in these parts of how Moro pirates used to lure their Spanish pursuers into tide-rips and whirlpools where small ships vanished with all hands.

Our course was now due east to clear the Sulu group. I sailed her all night, watching the lights of shore villages on Siasi pass and disappear over our quarter. The crew slept, exhausted after frolicking on shore for four days. They had been very depressed when we sailed, and I admired their spirit in coming along at all. They were leaving behind them all the world they knew, and their ideas of geography were hazier than those of Columbus. No other race of native among the Filipinos would have produced a crew for such a voyage.

In the morning the easternmost mountain peaks of Jolo bore due north, distance forty miles. The wind was light out of the north-west, the weather fine and we were alone.

Usually our boys sang and talked more than enough, but on that first day out of sight of land there was an eerie quiet and I had to urge them on. I understood now why daily dancing was compulsory in some old sailing-vessels; it kept the men in humour and from getting depressed. In the evening, I encouraged them to sing and play the suling, a bamboo flute of sweet tone, almost the same instrument as the Japanese Shaku-Hachi, which is played by the hooded Buddhist monks.

The end of our first day at sea brought perfect weather and a fair breeze. We kept slightly to the north of our course, east-south-east for Sangir Island in the Netherlands East Indies, north of Celebes. There was nothing in sight after the last peak of Jolo had dropped below the horizon.

Sahibad and I understood each other better now that we had started on the final lap of our journey. We had much in common, as we were the only ones with some sailing experience. He handled his crew with much more tact than I had done—which was not saying much—and gradually, something like discipline began to emerge. As far as I was concerned, it was now or never.

The ship's company was made up as follows:

A. Klestadt, Joint-Master and Navigator
Second Lieutenant Frank Young, Philippine Army, Joint-Master
Sahibad, Sailing Master
Ali,
Sabdal,
Ajijohn, } Crew
Manguna,
Dalil,

The boat could have been worked in all weather by three men, but we were eight all told. Only gradually did I come to understand Sahibad's insistence on such an unnecessarily large crew. Safety was their main concern. They felt that five of them would have a comfortable margin if Young and I should go against them. Easier working shifts and a hankering after adventure were other considerations. Ajijohn was the son of a well-to-do Moro on Sangboy and had never touched a rope in his life, Frank informed me, but he was an expert barong fighter and had come along solely as Sahibad's body-guard. Except for this duty, he intended to have a lazy and pleasurable trip. All this was told to me only after we had sailed, they would not have dared earlier. An end was quickly put to this comic opera set-up; on a small boat it is share and share alike. Ajijohn had to work, and he never had a chance to prove his skill with the barong either.

We now carried the following provisions, quantities being approximate only:

160 gallons water
220 lb. rice
200 lb. cassava paste
150 coconuts
80 lb. sugar
100 lb. salt
25 lb. mongo (lentils)
20 pieces tinned food (assorted, fish, corned beef, fruit)
3 lb. coffee
$\frac{1}{4}$ lb. China tea
150 pieces dried salted fish
1 small tin coconut oil, for frying
3 lb. "Purico" margarine, for frying

For our own use and for barter we carried the following stores:

2 hands leaf tobacco
3 cartons matches
40 balls washing soap

The valuable commodities such as coffee, margarine, matches and soap had been bought from Chia at Labason with the proceeds of the sale of "Maring". The twenty tins were, of course, only for special occasions or for emergency use, and our provisions should give us sufficient food for fifty days if properly rationed. Firewood was no problem, but the shortage of kerosene worried me all the time.

Our water supply was sufficient for less than a month, but I was confident that we could risk watering somewhere in the outer Indies. What would have been difficult single-handed in "Maring" was now feasible with the larger crew.

A routine of ship's life came gradually, very gradually, into being.

We did small jobs most mornings, a lashing here and there, or a new water dipper fashioned from a coconut shell. Sahibad made a cunning binnacle for the compass, using our hurricane lamp and a soap box. This had given us many headaches, because the binnacle had to conform to certain requirements: the card and lubber line had to be sufficiently well lit to be clearly visible, with a minimum flame to conserve kerosene; there must be no glare on the eyes which would impair night vision unduly; the lamp had to be easily accessible if required elsewhere in the boat; brackets for the compass box had to be fitted on the poop to assure proper alignment of lubber line with the ship's bow at all times; but most important of all, not a chink of light must be reflected either on the helmsman's face or on any part of the boat. It was a tall order, and the finished product was an ungainly big box, but it never let us down.

Regular watches were set, of four hours each. Both Frank and Sahibad could steer a reasonably accurate compass course by now, and the night, midnight and dog watches were kept by Sahibad, Frank and myself, rotating daily. After dark, I insisted on quiet and did not allow an open fire to burn—we never could tell whom we might attract, and such safety measures were easily taken. It is surprising how far a voice, or the creak of a chafing rope, will carry in a still night. I had found that out earlier in "Maring".

We looked forward with some impatience to every night-fall, and the safety which the dark gave us from interception by Japanese naval patrols or by stray ships. We sailed well away from the steamer lanes linking Menado to Zamboanga in the south, and Zamboanga to Davao in the north; but in wartime, patrols by sea and air took little account of regular trade routes.

The starry sky was beautiful and comforting on those warm nights, and especially when the stars' reflections shone out of the still waters. Night was the only time when I had any privacy; then the crew were asleep, huddled up in their sarongs on the floorboards. I smoked my pipe at night now, for we had a good stock of matches and I had come to like the strong black Filipino tobacco, cured at Labason by Mrs. Friend to our own special formula.

When the four hours of my watch were up, I would wake Frank, have a yarn with him and curl up in a cotton blanket, with a raincoat on top. The wooden boards of the poop then felt as soft as any mattress. Since leaving Labason, I had kept to the same place, starboard on the poop, a strategic position and the Captain's rightful place. Here I was protected on one side and aft, and anyone who wished to come to me had to pass the helmsman. In an emergency I was at my place and could keep an eye on the course and note down speed every two hours. I seldom slept longer than that, the waking became almost automatic and I dropped off to sleep immediately afterwards. The steering of both Frank and Sahibad had to be watched; keeping a compass course without landmarks is a matter of practice, and one is inclined to let the boat yaw or come up to windward in heavy weather, especially towards the end of a watch. Only when the weather was very fine and when the crew were in good spirits did I relax a bit more and sleep a full six hours.

Our progress on the third day was very poor, the run from noon to noon being only fifteen miles. We wallowed in an oily sea, the crew asleep under the kajangs which

161

protected the well from both rain and sun. And all the time I sweated over my navigation, making the traditional cross on my worksheets to indicate my idea of the noon position.

All was well on board now. The crew began to eat cassava, toasting the strong-smelling paste over a slow fire. But our water consumption still remained too high. We had used seven and a half gallons a day so far, which was too much, almost a gallon per man. The boys were made to stay in the shade of the awnings during the hours of greatest heat to prevent excessive perspiration.

After having watched our Moro crew for some time, what I had first discovered in July was confirmed, namely, that the superiority of these brown sailors to our own was something of a myth. In fact, a European could teach a Moro sailor a lot of things he had never heard about. A feature which was particularly surprising was their low physical stamina and will power. Allowing for the fact that my boys were quite young, mostly in their early twenties, I found they had a lack of physical resistance to such a minor unpleasantness as rain, and after every physical exertion, such as sail-setting or the shifting of our provisions, or bailing the boat, they needed a prolonged rest. On the few occasions when they had rowed in the Sulu group, it was for a few minutes only and I smiled now at their earlier statement that they would row the boat in a calm at sea! They had told me that at Sangboy to justify the large crew. They would no more row at sea than rope-walk.

Sahibad stood above the rest in every quality that makes a sailor. He was around thirty and had learned the lore of the sea from his father, with whom he had sailed since boyhood. I would not have minded going it alone with him. There developed a bond between us; but stronger than this were his tribal loyalties to the crew, for whom he felt responsible.

"Kakugan" was proving herself a most amenable ship, beautiful in a seaway and easily handled. The tiller responded to finger-tip control on all courses. I had to confess to myself that she was a better sailer than my well-beloved little "Maring" had been. There was a difference, of course; the simple sail plan of "Maring" was easily handled by one man and practically fool-proof. "Kakugan" always required much looking after, the sail was huge and its handling awkward in the extreme; she could never be made to steer herself.

To Western minds, "Kakugan's" rig, which in actual working resembled fore-and-aft rigging more than anything else, would be a cross between a lug, square and fore-and-aft sail. It was astonishingly well balanced, and the tiny rudder took care of the steering quite easily and pleasantly. The boat carried a correct amount of weather-helm at all times. Reefing the sail was accomplished by the simple expedient of rolling part of the sail around the boom, a sort of primitive roller-reefing.

The performance of the boat on all points of sailing was good, and I was astonished to see her lie five to six points to the wind easily, and without pinching. Strangely enough, running with the wind dead aft was not very satisfactory. The sail had a tendency to force a jibe, which in anything of a strong breeze would have had a disastrous effect, as there were no stays to leeward.

In the absence of all such aids as purchases, blocks and sheaves, sail-handling became a clumsy business. Staying, for instance, was a manœuvre of so much complication that it could be done only in light weather. Wearing was altogether impossible. Usually, if the sail had to be shifted, it was lowered and set again "on the other side".

To a Western yachtsman, ours was a primitive way of sailing. But surroundings and average weather conditions largely govern the evolution of any particular system of sailing, and out here, storms were infrequent and light winds usually prevailed. This fact, together with the large crews they carried, made the cumpit's clumsiness—which had the advantage of simplicity of construction—somewhat unimportant. A heavily sparred cutter would have been out of place here. Conversely, our good cumpit would have been a sorry sight in an Atlantic gale.

On the third day after leaving Manubul we had the best day's run of the whole trip, more than a hundred nautical miles. For almost twenty-four hours "Kakugan" fairly raced along with the wind on her quarter, bounding over a sunny sea covered with white horses. I hesitated to put the little cross where I thought it should go, but I had checked my navigation hour by hour. The landfall proved the run to be correct. How simple it would have been if I had had a log, but as it was I had to estimate the speed of the boat by the simple means of watching the wake, and counting the time it took an object to float from stem to stern.

In the afternoon the wind blew up into half a gale. The working log told the tale:

"Noon–6 p.m.	Course SSE, 4 knots.
6 p.m.	Reefed.
6 p.m.–Midnight	Course SE, 3 knots.
Midnight 11/11–3 a.m 12/12	Course SE, 3 knots.
3 a.m.–8.30 a.m.	Stowed sail and hove to in rising wind, letting go our anchor as improvised drogue.
8.30 a.m.	Rent sail trying to hoist it. Set to mending right away.
9 a.m.	Course SE, reefed, 4 knots."

I nursed her helm all afternoon and into the night, it was wonderful sailing with white-bearded waves rising. "Kakugan" proved a superb sea-boat and excelled with the wind abeam or aft. Even in the fairly heavy sea running towards 5 p.m. she never took anything but a few drops of spray over her bows, while her poop kept bone dry all the time. Reefed down, and in a rising sea, she lost much speed but kept gamely at it. We never for a minute lost our feeling of complete safety in her.

The sunset was wild and imposing, with a flecked sky of an unhealthy purple colour over black, foam-crested waves. The wind blew up some more after dark, and it became difficult to watch the rising seas while steering, so at 3 a.m. I decided to call it off, particularly as a stinging rain began to fall. It was surprising how cold one could feel so near the equator. All hands were turned out to lower sail and un-step the mast. While we kept her bows before it in the dark, the crew lashed all spars and such gear as had to be secured. Then, awaiting our chance, we rounded to and let go our anchor to act as a drogue, paying out the full thirty fathoms of warp. This kept her head up, and she lay drifting quietly in the trough of the waves, except for an unholy rolling movement, which was of no consequence. Two crutches carried for the purpose were now lashed amidships in the well-decks fore and aft and the mast fitted in them, forming a ridge pole for the nipah awnings, which were bent across and lashed down. The boat now was a decked-in little house with an almost waterproof roof, drifting across the angry sea. We all crouched under it in our sodden clothes and slept soundly and safe while the good boat looked after herself.

Next morning the sky was grey and the sea somewhat disturbed, and although we managed to cook our rice under the awning, we were almost asphyxiated with smoke. We had to bail for about an hour, as much rain had got into the bilge.

Towards 8 a.m. we made sail but tore a hole in it owing to the instability of the boat in the swell. This was quickly mended and half an hour later we were under sail again.

According to my reckoning, this was the day when we should see land, and I lived in anticipation of my landfall, always a thrill. A tin of sardines was offered as a prize to whoever first made out real land and not just another cloud bank. Around noon we saw it, a small dark cone on the horizon. Land was about eighty miles farther north than I expected. I soon realized that I had made a big error, caused no doubt by my ignorance of currents. What I thought had been the coast of Davao Peninsula, turned out to be Sangir, largest island in the group bearing the same name. Anyway, the error could have been greater, and there was no Board of Admiralty to court-martial and dismiss me.

We closed with the land at last light, anchoring for the night in the lee of a small, steep island. We could all do with a good night's sleep at anchor, after our first taste of five days of open water.

Next morning, we shifted to the island of Karakitang, our first call in the Dutch East Indies. The island looked much like the Philippines, only more deserted and wind-blown.

The crew were perking up, now that land was in sight. They regained much of their former cockiness and insolence and made fools of themselves brandishing their kris and barongs at a canoe-load of obviously harmless natives who came out to see what this strange craft was doing. Later on another canoe came paddling by, and we gave them some tobacco leaves in exchange for a few Dutch coins, which the crew kept. These coppers were their first experience of foreign exchange; they just could not understand that there were places in the world where pesos and centavos had no meaning.

We had to be off again, and our next leg was across the Molucca Passage, some hundred and eighty miles to the western point of Morotai Island, north of Halmahera.

We left Karakitang at night, course east by south, to a weak north-west breeze, and at one in the morning were thirty-five miles on our way to Morotai. A long swell came from the open Pacific, and strong currents were obviously at work, making for disturbed water. I had a feeling that we were being carried to the south-west by the current at a considerable rate, but dared not base my navigation on that assumption. If I was wrong, we would have been too far north of our landfall, and would be delayed by overshooting our goal. Unfortunately, the high islands of Sangir and Siao had disappeared in the haze astern next morning, so that I could not take bearings on them.

I should have preferred to sail along the west coast of Halmahera, but there the danger of Japanese patrols was doubtlessly greater than along the east coast. On the other hand, observing the huge swell running, I expected difficult navigation along the north of Morotai and the Halmahera east coast. These waters were exposed to the open Pacific and studded with many shoals and reefs. Altogether it was a difficult choice of evils, and I decided to make up my mind after we had established the exact position of our next land-fall.

These and other thoughts about the navigation and management of the boat kept me constantly occupied. There was nobody with whom I could share my worries, no one to turn to for advice. Although I tried not to let my anxiety show, for the sake of the ship's morale, I definitely lost my sense of humour for a time. Hardly anything made me laugh, not even the antics of gold-toothed "Mister Ali", the ship's cook and clown. Being rather an untidy fellow, Ali had, of course, immediately been appointed ship's cook in accordance with ancient seafaring tradition. He knew a little English and asked whether there were cinemas in Australia and, if so, how many centavos was the admission fee? He called me "Mister Al", and this name stuck, as the crew could not pronounce my foreign name. Ali took more liberties than the rest of the boys did, and his grimaces and antics sometimes relieved tension at critical moments. Nevertheless, I thought him to be quite a shrewd fellow and did not doubt that he would stick a knife into my back if it would serve his ends. These were mean thoughts I knew,

M

but there seemed a gulf fixed between Moslems and others, which nothing could apparently bridge. The missionaries who had lived in Moro country for many years had told me about this, but I had doubted their convictions. Now I saw more clearly what they meant.

It took us two and a half days to cover the one hundred and seventy-two miles across the Molucca Passage—fast sailing for a small boat. If it had not been for my constant nagging doubts about the currents, this would have been a pleasant cruise. The horizon was empty, except for fine-weather clouds sailing high in the sky, and watching "Kakugan" slide up and down across the long rollers, never faltering, was a constant delight.

While we were at sea, out of sight of land, the crew behaved pretty well on the whole and did what they were told. I had time now to study them more closely. Normally I was a peaceful fellow and respected the privacy of others as long as they left me alone, but here I had to know each man as well as I could. Any one of them, if not properly handled, could wreck the whole undertaking.

Frank Young worried me from the start. As with so many Eurasians, two souls lived in him, one tugging against the other. Of his basic loyalty and courage there was no doubt. His father, an American, who came to the islands long ago, had instilled in him some of those ideals and creeds for which America has stood in the Philippines. His schooling had been the best available in the islands, which was not saying a great deal by Western standards. From his mother came the Moro fighting blood, and it was natural that he should go for an infantry career. I believed his accounts of the fighting in northern Luzon, where he apparently did very well fighting successful rear-guard actions as a platoon commander.

But on this sea voyage, Frank's Moro heritage and family connections claimed him very strongly at times. He was often of two minds, a pitiable sight, which made me realize afresh the dangers of trying to mix East and West. His American education had not been strong enough to make him impervious to the mental pressure now exerted upon him by the crew and, being ignorant of the stern demands of deep-sea voyaging in small ships, he sometimes took the crew's side in an argument when I needed his support. But he could always see my point at least half-way, and the result was a floundering, searching attitude which was pitiful to watch. That he was as anxious as I was to get to Australia was the saving element in our crew situation.

I knew from the look on all faces that he often failed to translate correctly what I had to say to the crew, and they to me. That he did that to save my feelings only endeared him more to me, but it didn't help matters, neither did his equally likeable attempts to "sell" me to the crew as not such a bad fellow after all.

I could not help liking Frank Young and his quick and impulsive ways. But on this voyage I could not rely on him as I needed to. He was as suspicious of me as the rest, mainly because he could never quite understand my navigation, or my reasons for this or that alteration of course. To reassure him, I tried to explain what I was doing with pencil and paper, and with my compass. He pretended to understand, but I doubt if he ever did. He made the mistake of trying to pass on his knowledge to Sahibad and to the crew, in order to allay their suspicions in turn. This was quite wrong, for the crew had no chance whatever of understanding what was going on. Tedious argument and useless controversy usually ensued, which often taxed my patience heavily. I kept my own doubts and flounderings to myself and tried to put up a bold front, but it was often difficult.

Sabdal was the next on the seniority list after Sahibad, a good-looking young fellow, strong as an ox and Sahibad's right-hand man for sail-handling. Both Sabdal and Sahibad were intensely proud of having served terms in gaol for some attacks on Christian Filipinos on Mindanao. The charges, I understood, included manslaughter and arson among other things, but I was content not to learn more. Sabdal and I often got on very well together, we had competitions as to whose eyes could make out land more quickly, and he usually won. But in his moods, he was as bad as the rest of them.

Ali, cook and ship's jester, provided badly cooked food and first-class comic relief at times. His seamanship was nil, and his clumsy attempts at handling gear infuriated Sahibad and made everybody else laugh.

Ajijohn, whom the crew sometimes called Job, was an enigma. A small and lithe fellow of reticent behaviour, he was in charge of the ship's armoury and daily treated barongs and Sahibad's kris with stones and strops, giving them an edge fearful to look at. He never settled down to help with the boat's work, except for an erratic burst of energy designed to please me. He was a bit of a dandy, and always looked the most presentable of us.

Manguna was the baby of the crew, hardly twenty. A quiet and likeable lad of good family and our top helmsman. He spoke a little English, having had some schooling at Zamboanga. He could also read slowly and was the best spear-fisherman aboard, which was saying a lot. Manguna also obeyed tradition and did what he was told by Sahibad and by the rest. Nevertheless, I felt that he understood the reasons for my orders better than the rest of them, except Frank and sometimes Sahibad.

Dalil was without a doubt the black sheep. A warped character of shifty appearance, he made a champion sea-lawyer. He was at odds with all my orders on principle and constantly influenced the crew, who did not like him either, but listened just the same. His seamanship was barely average, and his relations with me were erratic. When land came in sight at the time and place I had prophesied that it would, he crawled to the poop, stroked my arms and legs saying: "Very good, Mr. Al, very good." Five minutes later, he would again glower and threaten. I believed he was a coward at heart, with all his threats and bullying. He was the only one aboard whom I never learned to like.

There we were, the eight of us. Often—especially at the most critical stages of our voyage—it was one against seven, or two against six at best. We were a mixed bag all right, but I never gave up my attempts to make "Kakugan" a happy ship, and for days on end I succeeded. Had it not been for Dalil, there might never have been any serious trouble at all. He was the bad leaven.

These were the good days on the way to Morotai. Navigation and working ship had become largely routine. Watches were shared between Young, Sahibad and myself, and the only one of the crew to take the helm occasionally was Manguna. I liked my night turns best of all. Then the crew slept and I was at rest. When the sky was clear I steered by the stars, checking with the compass every fifteen minutes and selecting a new one for a marker as they continued in the orbit from East to West. When near land, or in bad weather, I often steered the night through. Dawn was not as welcome as it would have been in peacetime, and long and tantalizing were the minutes before there was light enough to see that we were not in sight of a Japanese patrol boat.

After I had sat in the same position on a hard plank for twelve hours, from dusk to dawn, steering the ship to a set course, my joints became stiff and deep fatigue set in. I was often too tired to eat and only drank half a glass of water before huddling up in my blanket. Sleep came quickly and I did not wake until 11 a.m., when hot rice was ready and it was time to begin working out the day's run. But before falling asleep, I often felt that whatever might come in the future, I had known the proudest place a man who loves the sea can fill: the command of a ship.

THE MUTINIES

On 15th November we made out land to the south-east early in the morning. My supposition regarding a strong south-westerly drift proved to have been correct, for our landfall turned out to be the Loloda Islands, uninhabited rocky outcroppings to the south-west of Morotai. Our landfall being farther south than hoped for, we had to go through the Straits of Morotai, otherwise too much time would be lost working our way north round the island. We were looking for an anchorage near where we could water and caulk several leaks which had appeared near the mast step. "Kakugan" worked considerably, which in itself was nothing to worry about, but necessitated much bailing and occasional recaulking.

The crew had become more tractable now, their first trip outside familiar waters was subduing them a bit. Nevertheless, I expected trouble once we were near shore. We could not waste time, and the incident which had occurred near Karakitang was not to be repeated.

The weather was getting very hot as we neared the equator. As it was Sunday, we prepared mongo for breakfast and also opened two tins of sardines as a supper treat, but in the evening the peace was disturbed by an unpleasant incident with the crew during which I regrettably lost my temper. Ironically, the subject that set off the blaze was the same which had caused the mutiny on H.M.S. "Bounty", a hundred and fifty years earlier: coconuts. I was lying only half asleep and our evening rice was already cooking, when Dalil and two others foregathered on the fo'c'sle. They were not quite concealed by the sail, and I saw them chop up two nuts—our iron rations—and eat the meat with sugar. This infuriated me so much that for the first time I went off the deep end and cursed them freely in every language I knew. The boys dropped the nuts overboard, whether they were afraid or only startled at my fury, I did not know or care.

Next morning, in heavy rain, we anchored off a small village on the north-east coast of Halmahera in the sheltered waters of Morotai Strait. Here we took on fresh water from a clear spring and bathed. At sea there was no water to spare for such luxury, and the sensuous pleasure at having all the salt grime washed off by cool, clear water helped my morale.

We dynamited a small school of fish, an effective but not very sportsman-like way of replenishing supplies. We gorged ourselves on the fresh article and salted about a hundred. Not even in Japan did I eat such delicious fish. Mister Ali knew just what to do. A hot fire, a little coconut oil in the big cast-iron frying-pan and in they went, white fillets of firm flesh, just out of the water. What a change from the eternal rice.

These were the Spice Islands of old, the name by which the Moluccas were commonly known in the last century. But their startling beauty was somewhat lost on us, the strain was too great, we had to press on. From some natives we had received word in broken Malay, of which Sahibad understood a little, that the Japanese had a "kampong" in or near Tobela, about twenty miles south. They were reported all around, in Galela, Tandjong Lelei and on several other islands in the vicinity, even on very small ones. The crew were badly scared by all this talk. There were whispered words and bad faces. The atmosphere of evil and fear was so real I could have grasped it with my hands. Frank Young's transparent diplomacy in translating only confirmed my suspicions.

I sailed away from this idyllic spot with a sullen and scared crew, and that evening the wind blew up. We were in a precarious position, being driven on to the ten-fathom shoal along the south-west coast of Morotai Island in a rising on-shore wind. We attempted to tack for an offing but could not, "Kakugan's" drift being too great because of her shallow draft. Finally, we had to give up, and in the falling darkness we made for the shoal. For more than two miles the boiling reef lay directly in our path and it looked as if we were done for. With the wind blowing us along at the rate of five knots or so, our small ship would have been torn to matchwood on the jagged coral, which we knew must lie directly beneath the surface of that reef of white water. While only fifty yards or so away from the barrier we saw the entrance, a deeper passage of smooth water just wide enough to let "Kakugan" through. We made it and quickly shot into the smooth lagoon.

It was a wonderful deliverance, and Providence had again held her hand above us.

The lagoon, which encircles the south-western tip of Morotai, was studded with several small islands. We went quite close in-shore to one of them, anchoring over four feet of crystal clear water, in the lee of the land. Here we slept soundly all night, after the scare.

The next morning, 17th November, began peacefully enough. Although we were weather-bound we had plenty to do; the crew had to mend a large hole in our sail which we had torn the previous night when stowing it in a con-fused sea in strong winds, and also they had to fish our upper yard with bamboo strips, as we had heard some suspicious creakings there.

While the crew worked on the sail and spar, I did my navigation chores all morning. We had covered approxi-mately seven hundred and fifty miles from the Zamboanga Peninsula, and our destination was still some nine hundred miles away. We were almost half-way, the point of no return was near, and it was here that trouble struck.

In the afternoon I went ashore for a moment. The beach of this tiny islet was of very fine white sand with many curiously shaped shells lying about. The coconuts seemed smaller than in the Philippines and the trees planted closer together, otherwise this might have been any small island in the Sulu group. The few natives were very dark Malays, with here and there a sprinkling of more negroid types with dull and kinky hair—possibly they were Melanesians from New Guinea. There were a few grass huts to house the tiny community of fisherfolk.

We saw a plane going in a northerly direction; it was flying too high for us to see the markings, but it was presumably a Japanese machine. The crew were all agog and requested me to go and hide under the awning, so that my white skin—now deeply tanned—might not attract the plane's attention. As the plane was flying at about ten thousand feet, I refused this ridiculous demand.

The next day, 18th November, we still could not leave. It was blowing more than half a gale, with rain from the south-west directly in our path, and the wind raised an ugly hollow sea in these shoal waters. I was surprised to find such strong and sustained south-westerlies so near the equator at this time of the year, it seemed against all rules and regulations. But our anchorage was very snug, the best yet, and I was glad for the crew to have another half-holiday resting and getting things shipshape again.

After much coaxing and disagreement I made them clean the worst of the dirt that morning. The boat was stripped, her floorboards removed and our provisions taken from the bamboo racks. The bilge was thus exposed, and in it some long-lost friends were recovered, including pencils and a knife. Truly, bilges of small boats have a way of their own all over the world. The crew was then set to work with a bucket and the brush we carried, and the bilge and sides were thoroughly scrubbed. Provisions were then re-stowed. This by rights should have been done at least once a week. But the best I could usually do was to have the poop and floorboards scrubbed once a day with a brush and salt water.

Probably I should have let things drift, and said nothing, but that went too much against the grain. Moreover, I felt certain that this insistence on discipline and cleanliness was necessary if we wished to reach our goal in good health.

I really did not fancy myself as a "hard-case" martinet, and took no pleasure in my role of taskmaster. The fact was that, after more than ten months on the run, I was dog-tired and would have been only too happy to leave everything to Young or Sahibad and play the passenger. But I couldn't do this. I was the only person aboard with some little knowledge of navigation. My general seamanship I believed to be not inferior to Sahibad's, and for all their murmurings, the crew looked to me to bring them through. When we sailed out of sight of land, our boys were subdued and I could usually get done what was necessary. It was only near land and at anchor that they defied my authority.

During the morning of 19th November the weather cleared. We decided to sail, but waited for night when the small Malay settlement would be asleep and could not observe the direction of our departure.

Our stay at Morotai had been bad for the morale of the crew; bad weather always seemed to have that depressing effect. All morning they were muttering, and they made no attempt to obey my orders to get the ship ready. Vague reports had come from the natives about Japanese patrols in the vicinity, and now there was talk about not proceeding, and argument had broken out with great force. Dalil talked and gesticulated at length and finally broke into tears, and when I asked what the trouble was, all I got were evasive replies. Then Sahibad spent some time ashore talking with Frank Young, but when I passed them they shut up, and when I asked Frank what it was about he would tell me nothing.

If only I could have spoken their language that morning! Evil was in the air, the atmosphere of tension which had gripped everyone was so real it could almost be seen. But I groped in a fog. Unable either to understand them, or to make myself clear, I had lost the initiative.

The climax came in the afternoon. At noon, while our sails and spars were still ashore and the boat was at anchor in shallow water approximately fifteen yards off-shore, a black speck was sighted to the south-east and was quickly identified as a launch travelling at speed in our direction. I was alone aboard at the time.

When it was certain that we could not escape before the launch came up to us—it would have taken too long to step the mast and make ready—the crew, including Lieutenant Young, came running to the boat, grabbed their kris and barongs as well as the box with our home-made hand grenades, and waded ashore again. I was curtly ordered to stay aboard and could do nothing but obey. What was to be gained by their going ashore I still do not know, since the island was so small that one could walk round it in ten minutes, and the nearest land was too far away to be reached by swimming or canoe while a hostile patrol was around. It was quite clear, however, that the crew, including Young, were ready to abandon me.

While the launch continued to approach on a north-easterly course, I prepared my papers for quick disposal in a weighted-down biscuit tin always kept handy for the purpose. I called out across the water to Young and Sahibad, who had disappeared in the underbush, for someone to come and fetch the box to be hidden ashore. No one answered my hail, and Frank afterwards said they had not heard, although they could not have been more than forty yards away and the air was almost still in the midday heat. Since it would have been futile to throw the tin overboard in four feet of transparent water, I hid it among the coconut husks and firewood under the forepeak.

Meanwhile, the launch came on. She was a trim-looking boat of about seventy to eighty feet in length, powered by a diesel or petrol engine and with glass-enclosed houses, the type often used by harbour authorities for the ferrying of Customs officials. I could see the Japanese flag painted on her side amidships and flown from the stern. She now went through some strange manœuvres.

After drawing level with "Kakugan", but approximately eighty yards out in deeper water, she stopped, waited for about three minutes while a native from our little island paddled out to her and was taken aboard, leaving his canoe to tow astern, then resumed her former north-east direction. About two hundred yards farther on her course, the launch began to turn a wide circle to starboard, returned almost as far as "Kakugan's" anchorage and then again resumed her north-east course at great speed, this time disappearing quickly over the horizon.

What actually caused these strange manœuvres we would never know, but the following seemed as likely a conjecture as any: we were a suspicious object, and the native who paddled out to the launch probably told them exaggerated accounts of our numbers and arms, this sort of thing had happened before. The launch, patrolling well within Japanese-controlled waters, could not approach "Kakugan" closer because of her deeper draft. She was probably manned only by lightly armed natives in Japanese employ, or by Japanese civilians, as had been the Japanese custom around Zamboanga.

During the two minutes while the launch approached "Kakugan", I lived my life all over again. It seemed certain that I would be taken by the Japanese, and I knew what capture under these circumstances meant. Curiously enough, I felt no fear, only an apprehensive sort of curiosity, like watching a dangerous act in the circus. After many years, I can still see the scene, watching from below the forepeak of our boat: the white shore of the tiny island, the blue sky, the warm and transparent water and the pretty white launch approaching. There was not much time for it, but I did pray and my prayer was answered.

Frank Young afterwards told me that they were prepared to rush the boat from the shore if and when the patrol

178

should expose themselves by stepping from the launch over to "Kakugan". But if that were so, I wondered, why force me to stay aboard? If they really did plan to make a fight of it, would it not have been better to stay on board, where our close-combat weapons could do some good, rather than splash about in the water for fifteen yards and expose themselves to small-arms fire?

Other explanations, less charitable but more plausible, were that the crew hoped for a safe getaway, or for a bargain by handing me over to the Japanese. Be that as it may, the fact remained that I was compelled to remain aboard alone, abandoned by my two officers and by the crew.

As soon as the launch had disappeared over the horizon, my heroes came out of the bushes ashore and we prepared to leave in great haste. By 3 p.m. we set sail to a westerly wind which had sprung up shortly after noon and had freshened considerably until dark. I gave a course due east to sail along the southern tip of Morotai, intending to resume a south by east course after nightfall.

The crew had been silent all the time, and the shock of the encounter and our narrow escape was still in my bones when the main blow fell.

Young, speaking on behalf of Sahibad and for the whole crew, now informed me in words of defiance and finality that they were abandoning the journey to Australia and had decided to turn back and retrace their course to the Philippines. He argued that we had stuck our necks out far enough, and that there was no hope of escaping further Japanese patrols and he reproached me bitterly for not having taken cover when the Japanese plane had flown over two days earlier. I was advised not to attempt any interference with their plans, "for my own good".

Towards 5 p.m., while the ship was running well in the smooth lee of the Morotai shore, the crew, in defiance of my orders, altered course to the north-east to round Morotai and return by the same route by which we had come. I was requested to leave the poop and to consider that I was no longer in authority. When I refused, I was pushed down.

There now followed such hours of mental struggle as I would never be able to sustain again, not even to save my life.

I reasoned. I pointed out that it would take more time to return to the Philippines with adverse winds than it would to carry on to Australia, and that the risks of interception were equal.

I pleaded. I denounced the dishonour of their behaviour, in particular that of Lieutenant Young, an officer in the Philippine Army, a part of the United States Forces. By contrast, I held out a picture of wealth, honour and glory if they would persevere. I reminded Young of the obligations we had undertaken, and of the consequences of our non-arrival for many of his comrades.

I bluffed and threatened. I threatened that Sahibad's family and all of them would meet with certain death, as the guerilla defence force at Labason would never take their word against mine, and would never believe any explanation if "Kakugan" were to return to the Philippines without me aboard. What would the Panglima Sabdani say if they returned to Sangboy without his son?

I advised them to think things over and to be calm, as we were all still under the influence of our meeting with the Japanese launch. It was to no purpose, their faces remained hard and set, they were returning home.

Finally, I played my last and trump card. I told them with as steady a voice as I could that I would not navigate them home to the Philippines under any pressure or compulsion. I told them that no one else on board could take them back again. I explained that I would rather they cut my head off right at that moment than take me back to the Philippines and the certainty of capture.

I must have talked for well over two hours in simple

English, interspersed with my few Moro and Spanish words and with illustrative gestures. I believed they understood, even without Young's translation.

My stand eventually told. Frank Young, whose attitude in the beginning had been as uncompromising as that of the others, was the first to cave in. I firmly believed that he himself only took the crew's side after having been subjected to considerable pressure including threats to the safety of his wife and child back in Moro country. Afterwards, Frank admitted as much. About half-way through my somewhat impassioned speech-making he took heart and began to support me. By seven o'clock he began to weep, and shortly afterwards the rest of the crew were in tears, from strain and nervousness as much as anything.

By half-past seven in the evening they had agreed to give the southward trip another try and they swore fresh and tearful oaths of allegiance and faith.

No one was more surprised at the victory, as yet precarious, of persuasion over force, than I, and I felt I could hardly blame them for the action, Young least of all. I remembered how I'd had more than one attack of blue funk in "Maring" during June and July, but I could not see that I should have acted otherwise than I did.

Looking at the affair with the smugness of hindsight, there is no doubt about it, my lack of tact contributed to the trouble. I half knew it then, but did not much care, my first concern was to bring the lot of us through, and I had other things to think about besides worrying whether I offended a touchy sentiment here or there.

The real story of the conspiracy did not come out until later when we were in a calmer mood. A week had gone by, and Frank and I were alone, ashore on a small island, when he told me what a close call I had had. The crew had decided to turn back on the morning of 19th November—the day of the mutiny—without me, even before the Japanese patrol launch came into the picture. The reason the Moros decided to give to Sabdani and to my friends at Labason was that I had refused to go under cover when the plane had passed overhead two days earlier, thus "betraying the crew and endangering their lives". Frank said, and I believed him, that he interceded for me, but in vain, and that the plan still stood when we sailed at three o'clock in the afternoon, after the launch incident. Frank told me that Sahibad himself had been against the plan at first, but he had been persuaded by the pressure of the crew, led by Dalil.

It had been decided that I was to be decapitated, and the hour of execution was set for after sunset on that same day. They drew lots who was to do it, and the choice fell on Sahibad. He was to behead me with his kris.

Only now did I understand what all the talk and argument had been about ever since our "coconut incident" on the 15th and what all the looks meant, and the insolence. Frank Young had been in a terribly difficult position, being torn by his loyalty to both sides. All things considered, he fought a valiant battle.

At 8 p.m. on the day of the mutiny we altered course and once more sailed south by east. The wind held during the night, and by morning we were well to the south-west of Tandjong Lelei, hoping to make Sajang Island the next day.

The ship's company was in a sorry state of mind after the fray, and Frank, Sahibad and I worked ship and cooked unassisted. The excitement and the effects of moral pressure produced a curious physical effect on the crew. They lay in the bottom of the boat and hardly ate or drank. They did not even talk but just stared into space.

Again I steered "Kakugan" through the hours of darkness and lived on the tiny poop, which I dared not leave for several days. We never saw anything of our patrol launch again! For good measure I threw one of the Panglima's charm papers into our wake.

Contrary winds beset us during the next twenty-four

hours and a piping south-west wind all but stopped us from crawling south-east under reefed sail. The crew regained some strength now, after being all-in with head and stomach aches for two days. No land or ships were in sight.

Now we were nearing the equator and there was perfect calm during the night. The full moon lit up a peaceful world of stars and quiet waters, while the ship slept, and only then could I think of other things besides the business of running the boat. It was difficult to imagine that there still were such things in life as a walk through the hills, and music, and the company of good friends.

In the daytime I was always aware of the danger and the ugliness of our situation. The danger from the Japanese was comparatively easy to bear; it was an even chance whether we should be discovered or not. But the ugliness on board never left me except for those few hours alone at night. No privacy whatever was possible, and intimate fellowship with these fierce Moslems was rather more than I desired just then. Treason was always a possibility. It appeared as if there was a curse on these people; they had so little grace and tenderness and knew nothing of human kindness. All their talk was of kris, barongs, police, of killings and of the revolvers and shotguns they were going to get in Australia. Other people talk of their family, of their hobbies and jobs, or only of the weather, or the price of fish. Not so the Moro. He is easy to respect, but difficult to love.

And now it grew hot, very hot. We were only about eighty miles or so north of the Line and still there was no wind. Perversely, the rain which had so often annoyed us avoided "Kakugan" when we longed for it. Many rain squalls were seen on the horizon, but they all missed us, and tempers became frayed again.

On 23rd November another attempt at mutiny flared up. This time it was the lack of wind that touched it off and the crew, led by Mutineer-In-Chief Dalil, made to set sail for home again steering north-west to a light south-easterly breeze which sprang up shortly after dark. There were threats to me of "death right here", but I didn't think they believed it themselves. Their threats were like the falling puffs after a bad storm.

We were on top quickly this time, because Frank had been with me right from the start, and by night we had won them over, and once more we altered course to Australia. I felt that this uneasy truce could not last long, and I was desperately afraid that the next incident would finish our southward trip. But the Lord helped us and kept the north-east wind steady, and we picked up speed and made good a few more miles on our long trek.

I dared not relax now and steered all night, and again I discovered Dalil committing a capital offence. In the half light of dawn, after I had just taken the compass out of the binnacle and extinguished the lantern, Dalil sneaked up to the drums, fetched himself a coconut shell full of water and began to wash his face. No one else in the crew would have dared to do that, and he chose a moment while everybody was asleep. When I took him to task, he scowled at me savagely, but this was not a matter on which he could have won the sympathy of the others, and nothing came of the incident beyond Dalil's further ill-will towards me.

SOUTH OF THE LINE

The north-east breeze remained steady, the ship kept running fair and there was peace aboard for the moment. According to my reckoning, we were crossing the Line that day, 24th November. But I had many doubts, as strong currents were at work. All I could say with any assurance was that we were somewhere near the island of Gebe, east of Halmahera.

The vagueness of my navigating was a source of continual anxiety to me. I did my best, but had little confidence in my unchecked boat's compass and had no means of discovering the local magnetic variations. Moreover, I was insufficiently practised in computing the speed of "Kakugan" and in taking and plotting bearings. Our "charts" were not much help either.

The more intelligent of the crew, who followed all my movements with compass and charts with a mixture of awe and suspicion, acquired some rudimentary ideas of the vastness of the Pacific world. When I tried to explain the size of the continent of Australia in terms of islands they knew, bewilderment was complete and their curiosity was stirred to see such a place. Manguna was the quickest-witted of the lot and explained much to the others.

Again the north wind held all through the night. We had a glorious run and anchored in the morning close to one of the small unpopulated islands north of Kofiaoe, where we caught many fish of all shapes, colours and sizes, and the crew were happier. We saw a large four-engined plane going north, nationality undetermined.

Occasionally a large shark would give us the once-over, although we did not see many of the brutes and all kinds of sea-birds kept us company at different times, from tiny white gulls to large eagle-like rovers. One day Sahibad caught a little white dove-like bird which he intended to tame. I did not believe the poor creature would out-last the day, but it stayed with us right to the end of the trip. It would perch on the spars, fly away for a while, but it always returned to us. We took this as a good omen.

And on we went. The next night, watching a black squall approach while we were to the north of Kofiaoe, we stowed sail and quickly unstepped the mast. "Kakugan" was transformed into a small house with a nipah roof in the middle of the sea. The squall broke and water poured down in sheets, flattening the white-crested waves into a slower and more laborious swell, but fortunately the rain did not last long and soon we drifted in a near-calm among the Kanari Islands, north-west of Misool.

On 27th November we had a stroke of good luck. We found water on one of the smaller Kanari Islands. We dared not go to any of the larger islands for fear of bumbling into a Japanese outpost, and in the smaller places water was generally either brackish or non-existent. Since there was not enough water in the boat for washing of any kind and there were few rain showers, on most days we just had to let the salt and sweat congeal on our skins and put up with the itching. It was wonderful to find fresh water.

We also bought some delicious young coconuts from the natives, who were very dark with woolly hair and were dressed in G-strings. Probably they belonged to one of the New Guinea races.

Since their last attempt at mutiny, there had been a gradual but very definite improvement in the spirit of the crew. Even the poor progress of the previous two days and the great heat had not killed it, and with our fresh water and coconut supply, the feeling of the boat was much happier.

This improvement had not been achieved without some adjustments, largely on my part. I realized that I had gone very close to the limit in trying to insist on what I thought was a minimum of discipline and cleanliness, and I decided now that my chief duty was to arrive at our destination. With that in mind I accepted things which would have been galling under ordinary circumstances.

The boys were playing their suling flutes again, and they even returned to their long sing-songs of an evening. There could be no better sign than this. They made up the day's happenings into a drawn-out half-song, half-speech, and all joined in the refrains. Our favourite song was the story of some fraudulent prefectural election on Jolo Island in which the name of a certain Hadji Gulam kept on recurring.

I hoped that the good feeling aboard would remain with us and that the hundred miles on either side of the equator had been the turning-point leading to a happy ending.

I now enjoyed my night watches as never before, and

after so much practice, I no longer had any difficulty in staying fully awake for many hours on end. Sometimes after the excessive heat of the day, the nights were cool and soft, with a steady breeze driving the ship along at a slow pace; sometimes there was a bit of go behind the wind and she would cut the waves with a steady swish-swish and a clean-cut wake. One night I was startled as the boat ran through what looked like a pool of disturbed water, but when I saw that it was caused by a school of dolphins, I was exhilarated and wanted to wake Frank and the boys—but decided against it on second thoughts. The fat glistening bodies glowed like black lacquer in the dim starlight as they described graceful arcs over the water, in and out, escorting "Kakugan". They were so friendly, and playful, and so light-hearted. Quite different from us.

Always there were the stars to watch; the glittering and strange heavenly bodies of the Southern Hemisphere, some of them new and a bit frightening to the Northerner. There was the Southern Cross, with its two bright pointers, which made good markers for keeping course until they wandered off. Every night now, the Cross came up a bit higher, and I imagined that I could notice the difference. This was the clearest sign that after eleven months of wandering, Australia was becoming more of a reality, and less of a far-away dream.

On 28th November we anchored near some rocky islets to the east of Misool. The crew went fishing, their great passion! The bottom was covered with large shell-fish, which Ali pronounced "welly good to eeet".

We were now roughly six hundred miles from the north coast of Australia near Croker Island, and we entered the Ceram Sea with a good run of approximately sixty miles from noon to noon. Peace and good order were still aboard "Kakugan", and I was now able to arrange our days as I had always wanted to.

For me the day began at 4 a.m., when a very sleepy Sahibad or Frank shook me awake to take the watch. A few

187

yawns and a mouthful of water before settling down on the now well-worn crossbeam which served as a steering bench. A few questions on her speed during the previous watch, a short pencil note before the relieved watch curled up for sleep. Two more hours in the safety of darkness and then that anxious half-hour of twilight before it became clear that we were still alone at sea, safe for the moment. Every morning, as we approached what must be an invisible front line, this scanning of the horizon at daybreak became more intense and anxious. Sometimes a cloud bank would look like a smoke smudge, or a floating piece of wood like a patrol boat yet far away, and one's breath would stop for a moment. We were such a sitting duck of a target in daylight!

Around six, the clouds in the sky due east began to glow, every morning a different shade of pink, and the sea turned from dark grey to dark blue, growing lighter as the sun rose and gave warmth to the cheeks.

Now the crew would begin to stir, stand up, yawn, fold their sarongs away and look around the horizon, mostly for land. They would smile, glower or look indifferent, according to disposition. Early morning is indeed a testing time for human temperaments.

Mister Ali, of the golden tooth, would come trudging sleepily to the well-deck aft to light two fires, one for a pot of coffee, of which we would each have a coconut shell full, the other for rice or cassava.

By 8 a.m. I was relieved of the watch and performed such ablutions as were advisable with salt water. I had even come to like the strange mixture of toothpaste and brine.

At 9 a.m. I had "Consultation Hour" to look after the minor medical complaints. A bruise here needs a dash of iodine, or an ulcer has to be cleaned and bandaged afresh with any old piece of cloth which may be handy. In an extreme case of head or stomach ache, an aspirin is administered and gratefully received. The crew were very keen on "medicine", as they called every kind of treatment. If I was thankful for one thing, it was that we were all well, and that there had been nothing more serious than some tropical ulcers and bruises.

From then onwards to 11.30 a.m. my time was my own, and I usually wrote up my log and read my Bible.

11.30 a.m. to 1 p.m. was given up to working out the day's run and transcribing it on the worksheets, announcing to the crew the distance sailed from Labason and the distance still to be covered to Australia. Then I slept until 4 p.m., when the next watch was due. Our evening meal was around 6 p.m., so that the fires could be out by dark. After dark I quickly went to sleep to get a good eyeful before my next watch, this time from midnight to 4 a.m.

The routine of Frank and of the crew was much the same, although less rigid, and also less busy. They smiled at my fad for doing the same things every day at the same time, but I didn't mind that.

It was not always possible, of course, to maintain the same schedule, but there is no doubt that it is important to live by the clock when making long passages in small ships.

On Sundays now we had extra treats for dinner: a tin of corned beef or sardines, and in the morning a feast of coffee and the few papayas, which we had traded against some sugar at our last stop. Each one's share was more a reminder than a meal, but it relieved the monotony. Still, we lived well on rice, sugar and coconuts, although almost all our dried fish were gone. I discovered myself remembering delicious food I had eaten in the past: steaks, soup, or a piece of chocolate cake. . . . I made up my mind to have cheese and chocolate in Australia at the earliest opportunity.

The weather now became fretful and skittish with weak breezes, mostly from northerly quarters, and many thunderstorms accompanied by short squalls. This was near-equatorial weather. I remembered having read somewhere that the so-called "heat equator" moves north and south of the Line with the seasons. A steady north-east current saved our daily runs. We made approximately one hundred and twenty-five miles in two days after leaving the vicinity of Misool.

Our course took us near settlements on the west coast of New Guinea and on the east coast of Ceram where the Japanese were likely to have garrisons. But Young and I never talked about the one thing constantly in our minds—interception by the Japanese.

On 30th November, Gorong Islands, south-east of Ceram bore south by west, distance twenty miles, and we saw two ships pass to the north in the evening. They were close to the New Guinea coast and far away. It was impossible to identify either their type or nationality, as only the masts and part of the superstructure were visible low above the horizon and these were at times obscured by the light swell running. No noise was audible in the near-calm then prevailing, and no smoke could be seen. Our ship's company, including Frank, were certain they were American submarines, and submerged at that!

Relations between the crew and myself continued to improve. They were eager to do my bidding, and the strain between us eased. Whether I had broken them in, or they me, was largely a matter of viewpoint. No one had any more ideas about returning.

THE LAST STAGE

Tension now began slowly to grip the ship as we approached the last stage of our journey. Three men were constantly posted as look-outs. Even to think that we might have any setback became unbearable.

Our little bird of good omen, which had joined us near Kofiaoe, remained alive and well. The crew had named him "Bird"—just that.

The north-east current was almost uncanny. With only

a few hours decent sailing early in the morning, one day we made a run of fifty miles from noon to noon. Otherwise it was all calms and cat's paws.

We anchored in the lagoon of a small island, this time in the Watoe Bela group—I was by now quite sure of our position, as I had taken many bearings which I could line up and identify on my worksheets. Approximately three hundred and fifty miles now remained to Croker Island, nearest land off the Australian coast.

Sahibad was again very moody and so were the crew, and my confidence in them was waning fast. I had an idea that Sahibad was anticipating the changed balance of power once we were in an Australian port, and fearing that we might turn the scales and take revenge.

A northerly wind blew up and we should have been off. But the crew had gone independent and wanted to fish; so, taking advantage of the calm and tempting water of the lagoon, I had a swim and joined Sabdal and Sahibad reef-fishing with diving goggles. They were expert at handling a gun-like contraption which shot a barbed spear with great force by means of expanded rubber bands.

This kind of fishing is described in every travel yarn when the author finds himself in tropical waters. It was a remarkable experience and I wished that I had tried it earlier. Never before had I seen at close quarters the different shades of the water from the shoal to the edge of the deep, the coral gardens and fish of such fantastic shapes in all colours of the rainbow. My clumsy thrashing about in and below the water gave the boys much to laugh about. Anything to keep them happy and willing.

I asked Sahibad whether he was not afraid of the sharks which often play about in the lagoons. He pointed to the amulet around his forehead; it contained a powerful Moslem charm against sharks, in which he had complete trust.

Ali had caught two large lobsters, and Sahibad prepared a tasty mess from a globe-like fish cooked with coconut milk. Now that the trip was drawing to a close—we hoped—I handed out what little tinned food there was rather more freely.

At noon on 2nd December we got away at last and the southernmost of the Watoe Bela Islands bore abeam to port. But our progress was poor in a calm sea, and the signs of war were increasing.

Three groups, each of two unidentified planes, flying in an easterly, north-westerly direction, came over at a great height and, near some small islands to port, we saw an old-time cargo vessel with a tall, straight funnel either aground or deserted. She remained in sight for five hours, hull down. There was only one thought in all our minds now, and the hours of night were more welcome than ever.

It became hot, a still calm. The boat rocked and nearly threw her mast out. For a yachtsman, the way to hell is paved with oily swells.

For two more days we fretted about in light winds somewhere south of the Watoe Bela Islands, uncertain again of our exact position. The wind was faithless and fickle, what there was of it came from the wrong quarter, and in two days we covered only thirty-five miles. The current which had borne us along to the south-east now definitely left us, and we thought we were beginning to notice a slight drift towards the west. This may have been due to a branch of the Rossel current which, according to a small blue arrow on the map from the "National Geographic Magazine", set westwards across the Arafura Sea. The lack of information about currents defeated all my attempts at precise navigation.

Our water supply deteriorated both in quality and quantity. Although both drums were stood upright and remained covered with lids, bits of rice and other matter found their way to the bottom, giving the water an unpleasant flavour. It looked more like tea than water, and we wished that it were. Rust in one of the drums caused the discoloration, but I remembered having read that iron in water was healthy, and it certainly did us no harm.

Although the boys had caught enough fish at our last stop to keep us supplied to Australia at the rate of a fish a day, most of our salt was gone now; so we had to eat what we could all at once and throw the rest overboard. The rice diet was becoming a bit monotonous.

Early in the morning of 5th December a heaven-sent northerly breeze came up and stiffened to half a gale, and Sahibad pressed the boat all he could. The speed at times must have been around eight knots and I hoped nothing would carry away; we all crouched on the poop to balance the weight properly. The sea was not very rough at first, but soon we had to reef. Sahibad excelled at this sailing and showed up "Kakugan's" qualities with all the skill of a first-rate helmsman. His face was a study in concentration and joy in the performance of a good boat.

The hills of the Kei Islands soon bore on our quarter, at a distance of thirty miles, and by noon the next day we had almost reached our record of one hundred and five miles, established in the Celebes Sea early in November. We logged ninety-five miles from noon to noon. Our position was to the south-east of Jamdena's southern tip, distance seventy miles according to my reckoning. We never saw any part of the island. If my Dead Reckoning was correct, we were about one hundred and eighty miles to the north of Croker Island off Northern Australia. We steered south by east to allow for the current setting west.

During these last days the strain was beginning to tell on our tempers and we became quite unreasonable. When we speculated on what it would be like in Australia, our chief worry was what "they" might do to us and to our boat. We got very hot under the collar and swore that no pettyfogging official asking for passports or suchlike nonsense would be allowed aboard without our permission. And we were dead serious about it. The emotional tension of many weeks was bound to tell, and we quite lost our sense of proportion.

7th December. A good run again, eighty miles. The north-west wind held and there was no sign of the enemy. The crew again became frightened because we had been forty-eight hours out of sight of land.

Sabdal, who had the best eyes, sat perched on the fo'c'sle all day. Sometimes a cloud bank in the south looked like land, but it was still too early. We lived only for the landfall during these few days.

8th December. The fair wind remained with us. According to my reckoning, we were not far off land now. We saw another unidentified plane that morning, proceeding in a north-westerly direction.

Most tinned goods were now gone; we ate rice only. As a precaution, we also reduced our water consumption, although we still had approximately fifty gallons and had caught about five gallons more in a rain squall that morning.

On that day, 8th December 1942, I crossed the track of Lieutenant (later Captain) William Bligh, R.N., who had passed through these waters on his open-boat voyage to Koepang, Timor, in June 1789. He had always been my hero. Pleasure sailing in Japan with my brother, we used to play Mr. Bligh and Mr. Christian, and kept it up for days on end. My brother Eric, being the younger, was of course always Mr. Christian, and we had a lovely time bullying and shouting defiance at each other.

I had read every book about Bligh I could get hold of, and I had copied him in many ways on this trip. His insistence on absolute obedience, on cleanliness and on the observance of a strict routine had been responsible for the success of the greatest small-boat epic the world has ever known.

Now here I was, crossing Bligh's track in circumstances which were not dissimilar. But I was so much better off than he had been. His boat, when fully laden, had only four inches freeboard whereas mine had about twenty. He had

had only an hour or less to get his provisions and supplies together, whereas I had weeks in which to prepare. He had had almost twice my distance to cover, and much more of it in the open sea.

To me Captain Bligh will always remain one of the greatest among the great sailors. For the last century and a half, the descendants and relatives of the mutineers have tried to smear his character in book after book, but for people who like sailing in small boats over deep water, he will be remembered as the Captain who brought a handful of loyal men across thousands of miles of trackless sea and kept them healthy. Throughout the trip in "Kakugan", I had tried to model my conduct on his.

Wednesday, 9th December came up like any other in the Arafura Sea. According to my reckoning, we should see the coast that day.

The signs of land increased, so did tension on board. The water became more shallow and lost the deep colour of the open sea; a turtle swam by and three sea snakes, and a butterfly and land birds were in the air. But still there was no land in sight, and I worried again about my navigation. But I felt that not even I could be such a poor pilot as to miss the entire continent of Australia.

At three in the afternoon I woke after a short sleep to take the tiller, feeling very tired and weak. The crew were feeling much the same and were all lying on the floorboards. The wind was quartering and faint, our course south by east.

At quarter-past three black dots appeared on the southern horizon, they stretched out and became a connected line. Land in sight! The coast of Australia!

After I had satisfied myself that I was really seeing Australia, I sang out to the crew. They now became electrified, jumping up and down, embracing me, some weeping openly, including impulsive Frank Young.

I felt nothing at all. I had often imagined in my dreams

o

what this moment would be like, but the reality was quite different. There was no conscious sensation of exhilaration or joy, only fatigue and flatness. I felt terribly tired and wanted to sleep.

The transition from the sublime to the ridiculous was swift. Sabdal immediately brought matters down to earth by asking me for the deck of playing-cards which I had promised him on sighting Australia. This broke the tension, we all laughed, and never has a deck of cards changed ownership with greater satisfaction.

We closed with the coast late that afternoon, anchoring near a sandy beach. Our boys cleaned rice for the evening meal, and Ajijohn and Ali returned from spear-fishing with a small shark. Its flesh tasted quite good but rather strongly flavoured.

After eating, we went ashore and, at last, as I stepped on to British soil, I felt a great wave of relief sweep over me.

AUSTRALIAN LANDFALL

To say that Australia was hospitable on our arrival would be an overstatement. All we could see was a wide line of sand dunes and, behind them, underbrush and clumps of trees. There was no sign of human habitation and, although we walked some distance inland, we discovered no water. When we returned from our exploration, it was to discover the colossal tide range of Northern Australia—"Kakugan" was high and dry and the tide half a mile out exposing reefs with needle-sharp shells and coral outcroppings!

Rejoicings gave way to the realization that our troubles were by no means over and the crew plunged into a black mood. After coming from idyllic tropical islands, the desolate and barren landscape had a depressing effect on us all.

We could not risk sailing during the night in this water for which we had no charts at all—only a map from the

"National Geographic Magazine" on which the whole continent of Australia occupied six by nine inches!—and we slept badly because of overstrain and the bites of myriads of mosquitoes. Never before or since have I seen so many mosquitoes and flies. They crawled around the corners of our eyes and mouths and into our ears.

The most important thing now was to verify my position. I believed that we were a good way to the East of the Coburg Peninsula, due to my over-estimating the strength of the Rossel current. I had done this purposely, as it was a positive error. It would have been awkward to have been carried to the west of Melville Island, in which case we should have had to cover another three hundred miles of open sea to Wyndham. We decided to coast along westward until we could make contact with civilization.

For two days the situation remained critical. We had come so far and I was determined that nothing should go wrong now; so we sailed only during the day for fear of missing settlements and landmarks.

On 10th December we anchored at the mouth of an indentation, apparently cutting into the land in a south-easterly direction. We went in with the tide to explore and to look for water, but found only mangrove swamps and more mosquitoes. We were glad to get to sea again.

There were many sharks around, but poor fishing otherwise. Manguna speared a two-foot shark which we cooked. The men were quite unafraid to swim and fish in these waters, which was much more than I was. They put on their amulets and felt quite safe.

We crawled along the deserted coast for another ten miles, which was all we did during the whole day. The situation remained dangerous, the crew said that this was devil's country inhabited only by flies and mosquitoes—perhaps their consciences were bothering them.

Our deliverance came on 11th December when the Lord brought us to our desired haven, just as it said in the Psalm.

All morning we had been anchored off a point and had made sail around noon to a weak north-westerly breeze, hoping to sail close-hauled on the port tack across a bay.

At 1 p.m. we made out smoke near the shore and became excited, hoping to find at least some natives and fresh water. On approaching I observed that the smoke covered too wide an area for a single cooking fire, and feared that a bush fire was fooling our hopes. We anchored far off-shore, the tide being out, and I went with Sahibad and Frank to investigate the smoke. I had a painful walk ashore, cutting my bare feet on the many shells. As usual, our men followed and had their kris and barongs at the ready.

We discovered footprints in the sand and saw some people at a great distance making for the trees. We set out towards the place where they had disappeared walking over flat country with tall trees of a type I had not seen before—this was my first acquaintance with the ubiquitous Australian Eucalypt, or Gum—and found that the smoke came indeed from a bush fire. But although we saw a number of empty cigarette and tobacco tins in the sand, there was no one in sight.

At last, we decided that the people we had seen had probably been frightened natives who had mistaken our strange craft for a Japanese boat, and we turned back towards "Kakugan".

We were walking along the shore and I was feeling deeply discouraged about our futile efforts to verify our position and to take on water, when we heard a dog bark. Looking round quickly, I saw a very black native, tall and stark naked, standing beside a bush, spear in hand, some hundred or so yards away. We hailed him and he answered in intelligible English asking for one "boy" only to come forward. I went, feeling quite afraid. There could have been fifty men concealed behind those bushes, and I disliked intensely the idea of finishing up on an aboriginal spear.

Fifty yards from him, I made signs that he should lay down his spear and come closer towards me, indicating that I was unarmed by waving a handkerchief. The black man dropped his spear but did not advance more than a couple of steps away from his clump of bushes. I then approached him, we shook hands and I quickly dispelled his fears.

Our men came closer now, hands still on barong handles, and the native called his companions, a few rather dirty black fellows, two women and some children. The aborigine then told us about a Mission Station on an island a short distance away and offered to guide us there. We accepted gladly and presented him with some tobacco, rice, soap and matches for his people.

Before he came on board, a last comic opera scene among the crew had first to be acted out. Our black friend brought with him a huge grey snake, at least five feet in length, thick in the middle and quite dead. He said that this was his "tucker", or food, which he wanted to take along. Our crew were quite horrified and absolutely refused to let this naked savage and his snake on board. A compromise was finally reached, and the native left his snake ashore after we had assured him that we would look after his inner man.

We sailed at seven in the evening with high hopes, and at 3 a.m. next day, 12th December, anchored close inshore off Goulburn Island. We slept till sunrise, then proceeded to the Mission Station, and when at last I saw the red-roofed buildings, it was with a deep sense of gratitude to Him who had brought us here.

Some natives paddled us ashore where we were welcomed by the Reverend L. N. Kentish of the Overseas Methodist Mission. Our reception was wonderfully hospitable, and I felt humble and almost fearful at the miracle of my escape. The air breathed freedom; I felt a great lifting of the leaden weight of the Japanese menace—it was a year and two days

199

since they had dropped their first bombs on Manila, and I had made up my mind to escape.

I was now able to contact Darwin by short-wave wireless, and I established our position and identified our landfall, which was rather far from where I had hoped to strike the coast. My error was eighty miles east of Croker Island. I also discovered that we had landed on an aboriginal reserve where the natives live in their natural state undisturbed by white men except for occasional visits from patrol officers and exploring expeditions. We had indeed struck the farthest corner of Australia.

Everyone was wonderfully kind and considerate to us, including the smiling black natives of the Mission. The Reverend Kentish cared for us like a father. He took some pictures of the boat and of us in our ragged and dirty state, after which we bathed. And what bliss it was to let the soap foam and the cool, sweet water run over our sweaty and crusted bodies. Then we ate, and never did bread, jam and cheese, washed down with pots of tea, taste better. We slept all night in real beds with no watches to go, no reefing or sail stowing to do.

Our crew were given lodging in a separate house and were well cared for. But they were very frightened, partly because of the foreign surroundings, but more for fear of retribution after their mutinous behaviour at sea. Kentish, Frank and I did everything to calm their fears, but they judged things by their own standards and it took a long while to convince them that they would come to no harm. Frank and I agreed that we should advise the authorities at Darwin to disarm them.

The Reverend Kentish made the service in his little board church that Sunday a special occasion for thanksgiving. He asked me to read the Lesson, Second Corinthians, Chapter four, to the native congregation and to offer a prayer, which I did very gladly. Verses 8 and 9 seemed particularly appropriate and recalled memories in both Frank and myself.

"We are troubled on every side, yet not distressed;
We are perplexed, but not in despair;
Persecuted, but not forsaken;
Cast down, but not destroyed."

Our voyage in "Kakugan" ended there, on Goulburn Island. The trip from Labason to Goulburn Island had lasted forty-seven days, thirty-two of which made up net sailing time over a distance of one thousand seven hundred and sixty-six nautical miles.

There was one aspect of the trip in which I took some pride: we had arrived in Australia as healthy as when we sailed from the Philippines. There had been no sickness on board and we had not even lost much weight. There had been planned escapes by sea before, in this and other wars and from shipwrecks, and often there were frightful tales of death and disease and hunger in open boats—even of cannibalism. One thing which I had learned from all the books I had read had been confirmed by my own experience: when there is trouble with small boats at sea, it is almost always the fault of the crew rather than of the boat.

Word now came over the short-wave link that a flying-boat would come and take us to Darwin, and we left our faithful boat to the Reverend Kentish, who said that he could make good use of it. "Kakugan" had served us well, but she was rather tired now; the sail had become thin and full of holes, and during the last few days we had had to do much bailing. She had not been built for the sort of strain we put on her, but she never let us down.

On the morning of 14th December, a Catalina flying-boat sat down gracefully on the water not far from where "Kakugan" had been brought to the beach. A lot of gold-braided officers of all services poured out and gave us a close inspection. They asked me to show them the boat and when I did, they said nothing. Perhaps they were doubtful whether we really had come all that distance, but I had my worksheets to prove it. I surrendered these to the people from Naval Intelligence and got them back some months later together with a nice letter from the Director, Commander Long.

We all said goodbye to the Reverend Kentish and piled aboard. The Catalina took off with a roar and soon Goulburn Island was below and "Kakugan" a little black speck on the beach. After a few hours flying, we landed in the comforting presence of warships in the harbour of Darwin. During the flight, our Moro crew had been very subdued but, true to type, they were fascinated most of all by the machine-guns in the blisters of the Catalina. When the gunners obligingly fired a few bursts, their admiration was boundless.

VI. THE HAPPY ENDING

AT Darwin we were put in hospital for observation, but they found nothing wrong with any of us and we were allowed to go after a couple of days. The only casualty was our little bird, which had to be destroyed under Australian quarantine regulations.

We were then separated. Frank Young and the boys were taken to Brisbane, where I was to join them for a short time later, and I was made welcome at the headquarters of Lieutenant-General Herring, who commanded the Darwin district. The General was absent at the time, and the Intelligence Officer, Major Basil Hall, took me under his wing. He had me fitted out with boots and my rags replaced with fresh khaki. If they were suspicious of me at H.Q., and I knew they must be, they never showed it and I was treated like an honoured guest.

Being an escapee from occupied territory, I had a certain amount of intelligence value and, after a few days, I was flown out by special plane to Brisbane, where General Douglas MacArthur, Supreme Commander in the Southwest Pacific, then had his headquarters.

The Army quartered me in a good hotel, and for several days I was interrogated at headquarters on everything I had heard and seen in the Philippines and on my way south. I could give a few isolated facts about Japanese shipping, about the locations and strengths of some of their garrisons in the Philippines and about our own guerilla forces. But in intelligence work it is not the individual informant who counts, what he knows is only one small bit of the huge jigsaw puzzle.

I met Frank Young again in Brisbane and found that he had been given a similar reception. He had blossomed into

203

the full uniform of a Lieutenant in the United States Army, and two days later, at General MacArthur's headquarters, he was decorated with the American Distinguished Service Cross for the part he had played. He had thoroughly deserved his decoration, of which he was intensely proud.

Shortly afterwards we said goodbye; Frank was posted to a unit of the American Army and I never saw him again. But I heard later from an authoritative source that he was soon promoted Captain and was inserted by submarine into the Tawi-Tawi group of islands in the southern part of our old stamping ground, the Sulu Archipelago, where he did important and secret work with the guerilla forces for the rest of the War.

As for the crew, they too disappeared quickly from my ken. But before they did, I had my compass engraved with a suitable inscription and then presented it to Sahibad. He in turn gave me his kris—the one I was to have been beheaded with. All six of the crew were housed on the outskirts of Brisbane in a special camp reserved for Intelligence personnel. They had been fitted out properly, and the promises which Frank and I had made them had been honoured. When I was told that they were to be moved, I went out to say goodbye; but what finally happened to them I was never able to find out, much to my regret. It was all very hush-hush at the time, but it may be supposed that they were taken over by those units concerned with supplying personnel and stores to the many coast-watching teams which remained in Japanese-controlled territory throughout the War.

At headquarters I was told that mine had not been the first party to escape from the Philippines. Two or three crews had come out, including that of Captain Herndon, the American yachtsman I had heard about but never met at Iloilo. All these parties had come in larger boats than mine, and all had had a motor or engine of sorts. So far as I was ever able to find out, we were the only ones who did it under sail alone.

Some time later, I was told by Intelligence officers of the Royal Australian Air Force that shortly after we had passed through the area, the Japanese occupied the islands in the Arafura Sea in strength. They established bases on the Kei and Tanimbar Islands from which they set up a system of close patrolling and the R.A.A.F. officers gave it as their opinion that if we had passed through two weeks later, we should almost certainly have been intercepted.

At Brisbane I tried to persuade headquarters to organize an expedition to bring back the missionaries from their hideout on the Zamboanga Peninsula. I had it all worked out and offered to go as a guide. I felt certain that it could be done with one or two submarines, particularly as the coast near "Forest Glen" was practically uninhabited. But although I pleaded with some feeling and made a nuisance of myself, they would not hear of it and nothing was done, as far as I know.

My trip was over now, but the War was not. Escaping from the Philippines had been a personal affair, something that belonged only to myself and to my crew, who were no longer in Australia. Now I wanted nothing better than to stop being a lone and rather eccentric adventurer; I wanted to become part of a community, with men around me who thought and acted as I did.

And so I tried to enlist. First I tried the Navy, of course. But they would not have me, probably because I was not then naturalized. Perhaps they thought I would pour sand in the breechblocks of their precious cannon.

At last the Australian Army took me and I learned to wear the Digger hat—the noblest headgear known to man. Like everybody else, I enlisted as a private soldier; later I was commissioned and became an Australian citizen. I did nothing spectacular and served until the end of the War in Australia, the Solomon Islands and New Guinea.

My unit was the Far Eastern Liaison Office, F.E.L.O. for

short, one of those odd intelligence units which spring up in most wars. The story of this outfit, which was quite secret during the War, has since been told. We concerned ourselves with propaganda, with the production of leaflets inviting the Japanese to surrender, and their distribution via the Air Force. The unit was scattered far and wide over the south-west Pacific theatre of operations, and its various branches were not only engaged in leaflet warfare, but also in more tangible operations. There were deep-penetration patrols behind the enemy's lines in New Guinea, small-boat sections, and front-line broadcast units. I was posted to one of these latter sections because of my knowledge of Japan and of the Japanese language. What good we did only the war historian will be able to tell, but we had a lot of fun and occasionally quite a bit of excitement.

When the Japanese surrendered in August 1945 my unit was in the mountainous jungle of New Guinea behind Wewak, and we had a hand in organizing the Japanese surrender, and in the concentration of the defeated forces on the shore.

It was very shortly afterwards, either in late September or early October 1945, while lying in a Field Hospital in Wewak, that I received a letter from a brother officer who had gone to Japan with one of the "Prisoner-of-War Recovery Teams" immediately after the Cease Fire. In Tokyo he had met Eric, who, as a stateless person, had been under police surveillance but had not been actually interned.

I had few personal ties in Australia (I had discovered when I first arrived in Brisbane that my fiancée had made other domestic arrangements), and also had now heard that Eric was alive and still in Japan, it did not take much to persuade me to accept a posting to the Occupation Forces in Japan. And there I found Eric and heard his story. He had been lucky. Although he had been unable to obtain a visa and leave with me and his business had folded up, he still had

"Spray", and he had been able to sell her and live on the proceeds until he was taken under the wing of the Swedish Red Cross, where he worked on prisoner-of-war records and enjoyed a semi-consular status, which enabled him to escape the attentions of the police.

I stayed in Japan for eighteen months, part of the time as Investigating Officer, War Crimes. One day a file came to my desk marked "The Rev. L. N. Kentish" and I opened it with fear. The story of his end was tragic. While he was travelling in a coastal ship, the "Patricia Cam", from one mission station to another off the coast of Arnhem Land, a Japanese seaplane had sunk the ship. As the weather was clear and the water calm, the seaplane, observing some men struggling in the water, came down and took Kentish on board. He was taken to the Japanese garrison in the Kei Islands and after beatings and interrogations he was beheaded. The Japanese responsible for this outrage—a civilian administrator—was traced, tried and eventually hanged.

From the files of the War Crimes Section I also learned that several escape attempts in boats from the Philippines and from other parts of Japanese-occupied territory had failed. In fact, for every boat that got through, there appeared to have been two or three which ended in interception by the enemy. In most cases which came to my knowledge, the Japanese had beheaded the captured crews.

The time came to go back to civilian life. I became engaged again, and early in 1948 I left the Army and settled down in Melbourne, where I resumed my peacetime occupation. It was also in 1948 that Eric came to Australia and began an Arts Course at Sydney University, where he finished with a brilliant First in History and afterwards specialized in Far Eastern History.

The story is up to date now, and it has a happy ending. Voyaging in "Maring" and Kakugan" belongs to the past, but I often think back to those days, and especially I remember the many pleasant adventures I had and the good friends I made.

The Moro hat presented to me by the Panglima Sabdani still does duty in the hot summer sun on Melbourne beaches. Sahibad's kris gets a polish and an oiling to keep it bright and shiny, and my wife uses my own bolo to split kindling and cut up the cat's dinner.

The present from the Reverend Davis is now our family Bible; two entries in it record the birth dates of our sons. The middle name of the older boy is Bligh.